Sustainable Operations and Closed-Loop Supply Chains

Sustainable Operations and Closed-Loop Supply Chains

Second Edition

Gilvan C. Souza

BUSINESS EXPERT PRESS

Sustainable Operations and Closed-Loop Supply Chains, 2e
Copyright © Business Expert Press, LLC, 2018.

First published in 2018 by
Business Expert Press, LLC
222 East 46th Street, New York, NY 10017
www.businessexpertpress.com

ISBN-13: 978-1-94709-866-4 (paperback)
ISBN-13: 978-1-94709-867-1 (e-book)

Business Expert Press Supply and Operations Management Collection

Collection ISSN: 2156-8189 (print)
Collection ISSN: 2156-8200 (electronic)

Cover and interior design by S4Carlisle Publishing Services
Private Ltd., Chennai, India

First edition: 2018

10 9 8 7 6 5 4 3 2 1

Printed in the United States of America.

Abstract

This book is targeted to MBA students, executive MBA students, and middle to upper level managers in general (especially in executive programs). The book can be viewed as firm's journey toward sustainability, starting from zero. A firm that wants to be sustainable considers the triple bottom line when making decisions: it considers economic (profit), environmental (planet), and social (people) impacts when making decisions. By focusing on the triple bottom line (3Ps), the firm ensures a steady supply of inputs such as raw materials and labor. The first step toward sustainability is aimed at *reducing waste* in operations, with the help of such tools as lean and six-sigma (Chapter 3). The firm then performs a life cycle assessment (LCA) for each of its main products and processes. LCA is a methodology designed to assess the environmental impact (such as energy consumption and toxicity) of a product or process through its life cycle: raw material extraction, transportation, manufacturing, packaging and distribution, use by consumers, and end-of-life. With a better understanding of the major impacts, the firm then implements actions that reduce its environmental impact (which in many cases also improves the economic bottom line), that is, the firm aims to be *eco-efficient*. Examples here include 3R (reduce, reuse, recycle) initiatives, implementing an ISO 14000-certified environmental management system, reducing the firm's carbon footprint through energy sourcing from renewable sources, and green buildings, such as LEED-certified buildings (chapters 4 and 10).

The final step in the journey toward sustainability is to *close the loop*. To close the loop, the firm starts by designing efficient packaging, designing products for multiple life cycles (as in design for remanufacturing), or designing products according to a Cradle-to-Cradle® philosophy, which ensures no use of toxic materials, ease of disassembly, and 100% upcyclability (Chapter 5). A firm that wants to close the loop may consider a servicizing model, where the firm sells a service as opposed to a product (Chapter 6). The firm must design its closed-loop supply chain, which includes a logistic network to collect products post-consumer use—in some cases, mandated by take-back legislation (chapter 2); in other cases a result of its servicizing model—remanufacture or recycle them, and remarket remanufactured products (Chapter 7). Finally, a firm does not operate in isolation, so it should also implement sustainability in its supply chain. It is thus important to understand ecolabels, and the role of independent and credible third-party certifications (Chapter 8). Finally, the book concludes with a chapter dedicated to the other P of sustainability—people, with some examples of firms that invest heavily in the social bottom line, and the concept of shared value creation (Chapter 9).

Keywords

carbon footprint, circular economy, closed-loop supply chains, Cradle-to-Cradle design, design for environment, ecolabels, environmental product differentiation, green supply chains, ISO 14000, lean manufacturing, leasing, LEED, life cycle assessment (LCA), remanufacturing, renewable energy, shared value creation, Sustainable operations, take-back legislation.

Contents

CHAPTER 1

Introduction to Sustainability and Closed-Loop Supply Chains

1.1 Motivation and Trends

According to Esty and Winston,[1] the top 10 environmental issues facing humanity include: climate change, energy, water, biodiversity and land use, chemicals toxins and heavy metals, air pollution, waste management, ozone layer depletion, sustainability of oceans and fisheries, and deforestation. A quick scan of the popular press reveals that the top two issues (climate change and energy) receive considerable attention, whereas landfill and depletion of natural resources only indirectly make Esty and Winston's top 10 list, under "waste management." Landfilling and depletion of natural resources, however, are critical to the sustainability of manufacturing firms. In a traditional supply chain, materials are extracted from the earth, processed, and used in the production of components. These components are assembled into a final product, which is distributed through different channels to reach consumers. After use, most of these products end up in a landfill. One person in the United States generates about 4.4 lbs of solid waste per day; 20 percent of that waste can be categorized as durable goods. Many materials in durable goods are non-renewable (such as zinc), even though recycling rates average 18 percent by weight for durable goods in the United States. At current rates of depletion, some predict that we may run out of zinc by 2037.[2] Simply put, without a steady supply of raw materials, manufacturing is not sustainable.

Electronic products, in particular, illustrate the issues with the sustainability of current business practices. According to the EPA, the United States generated 3.14 million tons of electronic waste (e-waste) in 2013. About 40 percent of e-waste is recycled, with the remainder trashed in landfills or incinerators.[3] Of the e-waste eventually recycled, some are shipped to developing countries for processing, although estimates vary between a mere 0.13 percent (International Trade Commission) and 10–40 percent (United Nations). This overseas shipment of e-waste is a gray legal area, as international treaties prohibit shipment of toxic waste across countries (and electronic waste is considered toxic, due to significant amounts of lead, mercury, cadmium, and other chemicals). Consumers typically replace their cell phones in the United States every two years (a standard contract with wireless carriers). In 2012, 140 million cell phones were thrown away, ending up in landfills in the United States, although there is a significant growth in the second-hand smartphone market.[4] These statistics have not been ignored by policy makers, who have been and are devising take-back legislation for electronic waste (e-waste), which holds manufacturers responsible for collection and environmentally responsible recycling of electronic products post-consumer use; this is a topic of Chapter 2 in this book.

Global warming has prompted some countries to devise legislations targeted at reducing the level of greenhouse gas emissions. The European Union Emission Trading Scheme (EU ETS) was the first large greenhouse gas emissions trade scheme in the world, established in 2005, and it regulates more than 10,000 installations with a net heat excess of 20MW in the energy and some industrial sectors that are heavy emitters of CO_2 (such as cement, steel, paper and pulp, aluminum, and chemicals) collectively responsible for close to 50 percent of the EU's CO_2 emissions. The government (each member state in the EU, such as Germany) issues each heavy emitter a number of emission allowances (allowing it to emit a certain amount of CO_2 per year); these facilities can then buy and sell these allowances in a market place. This provides incentives for these facilities to reduce their CO_2 emissions, due to its market-based economic value. The amount of allowances issued by the government determines the economic value of CO_2, and consequently the resulting levels of CO_2 actually emitted. As a historical note, this type of legislation, known as cap-and-trade, has also been implemented in the United States to decrease the amount of SO_2 emissions, in order to mitigate the problem of acid rain. Thus, firms under direct regulation of CO_2 in the EU must track their emissions. However, it is likely that cap-and-trade (or another type of legislation such as a carbon tax) will spread around the world, including in the United States. Many firms also view lower carbon emissions as a sign of higher efficiency in their processes, since energy consumption is directly correlated with carbon emissions. Efficiency means lower costs, and as a result, proactive firms take steps toward tracking and reducing their CO_2 emissions. Carbon footprinting is addressed in Chapter 3.

Another trend in environmental sustainability concerns labels associated with green products or facilities. For example, Walmart's concern for the sustainability of fisheries (and hence its future supply of fish) led it to target 100 percent of its farmed and wild seafood to be Marine Stewardship Council (MSC) certified; in 2017, this figure was in excess of 90 percent in the United States[5] Green buildings provide savings in energy consumption (through smart appliances, use of natural light and smart lighting), and water consumption (through rainwater capture and water-efficient fixtures), although a significant portion of green building savings, which are used to justify such investments, come in the form of enhanced worker productivity.[6] The Certification of green buildings via the Leadership in Energy and Environmental Design (LEED) rating system, promoted by the U.S. Green Building Council is being adopted rapidly: The number of LEED certified buildings grew from 11 in late 2000 to 1000 in late 2005 to 37,300 in 2017.[7] As an example, the Empire State Building was retrofitted, reaching energy consumption savings of 38 percent, and awarded Gold LEED Certification in September of 2011. More details on LEED Certification are discussed in Chapter 4, and sourcing green products is addressed in Chapter 8.

1.2   What Is Sustainability?

In this book, we take an operations and business perspective on sustainability. A sustainable operation is one that can be carried on *ad infinitum*.

As a result, a sustainable operation takes into account the 3Ps of sustainability when carrying out its decisions:

- *Profit.* A sustainable operation has to be profitable. Businesses are not philanthropic institutions (although they can carry out philanthropic activities).
- *People.* The operation has to be satisfactory to its stakeholders: shareholders (naturally), employees (since they carry out the operations), customers (as they drive revenues), governments, and communities where it operates (as this is the source of future and current customers and employees).
- *Planet.* Material resources necessary to carry out operations can be sourced *ad infinitum*, and outputs of the operation preserve the resource base (i.e., no pollution).

Another way to put this is—a sustainable operation considers the triple bottom line when carrying out its decisions: economic (profit), social (people), and environmental (planet). When Walmart made its decision to source 100 percent of its wild seafood MSC certified, it considered the triple bottom line: economic (since fish caught in a sustainable manner guarantees Walmart's future supply and consequently future revenues), social (since fish caught in a sustainable manner guarantees the livelihood of fish farmers for future years), and environmental (since fish caught in a sustainable manner avoids the depletion of fisheries). In this book, we will focus primarily on the economic and environmental aspects of sustainability, although Chapter 9 is dedicated exclusively to the social aspect of sustainability. There are several reasons for this focus:

- There is significant science behind many of the concepts of environmental sustainability: lean and six-sigma (Chapter 3), life-cycle assessment (LCA), and carbon footprinting (Chapter 4), design for environment (covered in Chapter 5), remanufacturing (Chapter 7), and renewable energy (Chapter 10). Other topics in environmental sustainability include legal and financial issues (such as environmental legislation, Chapter 2, and leasing, Chapter 6), and strategic issues (environmental product differentiation,

Chapter 8), which complement and support other disciplines in business education.

- In contrast, the social aspect of sustainability is taught primarily through examples. Although the examples (some of which are covered in Chapter 9) are interesting, there is arguably "more meat," from a teaching and learning in the classroom perspective, in the environmental rather than the social aspect of sustainability.

- As we argue in Chapter 9, a profitable firm that is committed to environmental sustainability positively impacts communities, so the social aspect of sustainability is intertwined with the environmental and economic aspects of sustainability.

Closed-loop supply chains are a key aspect of environmental sustainability; we introduce this topic next.

1.3   What Is a Closed-Loop Supply Chain (CLSC)?

In a regular (forward) supply chain, the predominant flow of materials and products is "forward." The supply chain for beer, for example, includes procurement of beer ingredients such as yeast, barley, hops, and water; beer preparation through mixing and fermentation of ingredients; bottling, which could be done in a separate facility; shipment to national beer distributors, then to regional distributors and finally to retail stores, where beer is sold. In reverse supply chains, the flows of products are in the opposite direction, from consumers to producers. As an example, the reverse supply chain for beer cans involves collection of used beer cans, consolidation in intermediate storage points, and shipment to aluminum producers and/or recyclers. The term *closed-loop supply chain* (CLSC) indicates a supply chain where there is a combination of forward and reverse flows, such that these two types of flows may impact each other, and may thus require some level of coordination.

As an example of CLSC, consider the supply chain for diesel engines and parts for Cummins (Figure 1.1). Figure 1.1 depicts representative flows in this supply chain; the flows are differentiated between forward and reverse flows. Forward flows consist of new parts and/ or engines, and reverse flows consist of used parts and/or engines, and remanufactured parts or engines. Remanufacturing (or refurbishing) is the process of restoring a used product (i.e., post-consumer use) to a common operating and esthetic standard. For a diesel engine or module, remanufacturing consists of six different steps: (i) full disassembly, (ii) cleaning of each part (often through multiple sequential techniques), (iii) making a disposition decision for each part (keep for remanufacturing or dispose the part for materials recycling), (iv) remanufacturing (value-added work that restores functionality and appearance similar to a new part), (v) re-assembly, and (vi) testing.

New engines are produced and assembled from new parts, some of which originate from Cummins' suppliers, who also supply the firm's distribution center with spare parts. New engines are shipped to a main distribution center, from where they are then shipped to several regional distribution centers (not depicted in Figure 1.1), and from there to over 3,000 dealers in North America. Customers buy new (or remanufactured) diesel engines or engine modules. They receive a dollar credit from returning the old engine or module upon purchasing a new (or remanufactured) engine or module; the dollar credit can be as high as 30 percent of the purchase price. A remanufactured module or engine typically sells at a 35 percent discount relative to its corresponding new counterpart. Used modules or engines are shipped from dealers to one of several consolidation points in North America (not depicted in Figure 1.1), and from there to Cummins' main used products depot. At the depot, customers are given the proper credit for returning the used module or engine; engines and modules are then shipped to one of two plants (or put into inventory for later shipment when needed): engine remanufacturing (plant A) or module remanufacturing (plant B). Remanufactured engines are shipped from plant A to the main distribution center, joining new engines or parts for distribution to dealers. Remanufactured modules are shipped from plant B to the distribution center or to remanufacturing plant A. Used parts that do not complete the remanufacturing process are sold to recyclers. Used products are typically referred to as returns or cores.

The supply chain in Figure 1.1 illustrates two major *disposition* decisions for cores: remanufacturing and recycling. In addition to land-filling—an option that is illegal for some products in some jurisdictions (e.g., electronic equipment cannot be landfilled in some U.S. states such as California, Maine, Massachusetts, and Minnesota)—disposition decisions for product returns include:

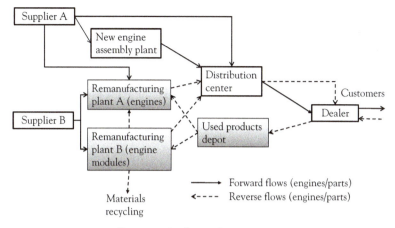

Figure 1.1 Closed-loop supply chain for Cummins (simplified).

- *Incineration.* Incineration reduces the amount of solid waste going to landfills, and it may be an attractive option for products or materials where recycling is difficult or uneconomical. In addition, incineration is commonly used for energy recovery. For example, Denmark incinerates about 60 percent of its municipal solid waste toward energy recovery. On the other hand, incineration may increase the amount of toxic emissions such as mercury, and is therefore regulated.

- *Recycling.* Recycling means material recovery, and it is an attractive option for products where returns have little economic value due to technological obsolescence (e.g., old computers), or are in poor quality condition (e.g., product returns heavily damaged during transportation). Recycling can be mandated by take-back legislation: in the Netherlands, 85 percent of the weight of each car at the end of its life needs to be recycled (as opposed to landfilled or incinerated); for electronic equipment, the current mandated recycling target is about 65 percent in the EU. We discuss take-back legislation in Chapter 2.

- *Parts Harvesting.* Here, the firm recovers selected parts from a product return for use in warranty and service contracts. When the part is subject to wear and tear, as is common in mechanical components, this option is viable if the product has been lightly used such as consumer returns. Otherwise, for electronic components, this is a common disposition option.

- *Remanufacturing.* this is a value-added operation as illustrated in the Cummins example, and it can be the most profitable disposition decision.
- *Resale (as-is).* this can happen if a secondary market for the used product exists, such as is the case with used cars, and some standard IT equipment.

Figure 1.1 illustrates a CLSC where the main source of cores are end-of-use returns, where the product has undergone a full cycle of use with a customer, but the product still has significant value left for recovery. In addition to end-of-use returns, there are end-of-life returns, which are products that have reached the end of their useful life, mostly due to obsolescence, and whose main disposition decision is recycling; examples include very old computers, monitors, VCRs, and very old cars. Finally, there are consumer returns, which are products that have undergone little or no use by consumers—they are returned by consumers to retailers as a result of liberal returns policies by powerful retailers primarily in North America; most consumer returns are not defective. For example, about 80 percent of deskjet printers returned to retailers by consumers in the United States were not defective: reasons for return include remorse, and lack of product fit with consumer needs.

CLSCs will be discussed in more detail in chapters 5–7, since they constitute a critical characteristic of a truly sustainable operation, as we discuss next.

1.4   A Firm's Journey Toward Sustainability

Suppose you are approached by a senior executive of a medium- to large-sized firm, with the following question: "We've heard much about sustainability, but I believe our company is not doing a whole lot in that space. What is the roadmap for us to become more sustainable?" This book aims to answer that question, providing a step-by-step path, with appropriate tools in each step of the path. The path is shown in Figure 1.2.

Pollution and waste reduction
- Reduce waste during product manufacturing & service delivery
  - Lean manufacturing
  - Six-sigma

Eco-efficiency
- Reduce consumption of energy and materials in processes: 3R
  - Reduce consumption
  - Reuse
  - Recycle

Closing the loop
- Minimize environmental impact of product through its life cycle (design, manufacturing, distribution, use, end-of-life and disposal)
  - Closed-loop supply chains and remanufacturing
  - DFE: Design for environment & cradle-to-cradle design

Figure 1.2 The path to a sustainable operation.

The first step toward sustainability is to **reduce pollution and waste generated by the firm's operations.** Popular and widespread popular process improvement methodologies, such as lean and six-sigma, are appropriate tools here. Firms implementing lean have reported significant improvements in areas such as scrap and rework reduction (which clearly decreases energy and material consumption), and inventory reduction (which reduces energy consumption), in addition to common operating metrics such as cycle time. Six-sigma aims at reducing variability in processes, which also reduces scrap and rework, for example.

With lean and/or six-sigma fully implemented, the firm performs a LCA for each of its main products and processes. LCA is a methodology designed to assess the environmental impact (e.g., energy consumption) of a product or process, from raw material extraction to production (in its different stages), packaging, distribution, consumer use, and end-of-life/disposal. With a better understanding of the major impacts, the firm can then target actions designed to reduce the firm's environmental impact (which in most cases also improves the economic bottom line), that is, the firm aims for **eco-efficiency**. Examples of tools here include 3R (reduce, reuse, recycle) initiatives, reducing the carbon footprint with clean and renewable energy sources, retrofitting/constructing green buildings (e.g., LEED-certified buildings), and implementing certain Design for the Environment (DfE) protocols, such as those aimed at designing products with low energy consumption, or reduced packaging.

The final step in the journey toward sustainability, which is the ultimate goal, is to **close the loop**. To close the loop, the firm starts by designing products for multiple life cycles (as in design for remanufacturing), or products designed according to the Cradle-to-Cradle® philosophy that ensures ease of disassembly and 100 percent recyclability (up-cycling as opposed to down-cycling), in addition to non-use of materials known to be toxic to humans or the environment. To close the loop, Cummins (Figure 1.1) designs engines that can be remanufactured (i.e., "sturdy" designs for multiple life cycles), has a reverse logistics network to handle used products (with collection of used engines at dealers for subsequent shipment to Cummins), has developed a remanufacturing process that guarantees that remanufactured engines operate "like new," and has developed a remarketing strategy, through pricing and warranties, to ensure that customers buy remanufactured engines.

1.5   Organization of This Book and Target Audience

This book was written from the author's experience in teaching a sustainable operations MBA elective in the Kelley School of Business at Indiana University since 2010. Although case studies are a useful tool in teaching, the author feels that a compact (but reasonably comprehensive) summary of the topics and issues of sustainability—from an operations standpoint—are just as useful, so that students get the "big picture." For example, many faculty members have taught DfE through the Harvard case of Herman Miller.[8] DfE, however, does not mean exclusively the cradle-to-cradle design protocol adopted by Herman Miller in the design of its Mirra chair, as detailed in that case. There is also design for remanufacturing, and there are other design protocols focused on eco-efficiency, and these concepts are explained in Chapter 5. Thus, the book's main target audience is students in elective MBA or undergraduate courses in sustainability. Given its relatively short length, the book could also be used in executive education, particularly considering that the chapters are self-contained for the most part. It can be complemented by case studies, some of which are discussed throughout.

The chapters follow the sequence of the path in the framework presented in Figure 1.2, except for chapters 2, 9, and 10.

Chapter 2 provides an overview of take-back legislation. This topic was included in the book because many countries (such as those in the EU, China, Japan, and Korea), and several states in the United States have adopted take-back legislation, which assigns responsibility for environmentally friendly disposal (i.e., recycling) of used products, post-consumer use, to manufacturers. This type of legislation has a significant impact on the operations of impacted firms, particularly those that manufacture electronic products. Chapter 9 is dedicated to the social aspect of sustainability, including an analysis of the stakeholders impacted by the firm's operations, as well as illustrating the concept of shared value creation.

Chapter 3 starts the path of Figure 1.2, and covers lean and six-sigma. The chapter starts by describing the seven forms of waste, and the overall philosophy of lean manufacturing. It then proceeds by providing a description of some tools in lean: pull processes, set-up time reduction, value stream mapping, 5S, and layout redesign. Then, the DMAIC process of six-sigma is presented, including the similarities and differences with respect to lean. Finally, the chapter concludes by providing the link between lean, six-sigma, and sustainability.

Chapter 4, the longest, is dedicated to eco-efficiency, the second step in the path of Figure 1.2. The first part of the chapter explains LCA in some detail, including several examples. The second part of Chapter 4 explains carbon footprinting, which is the process of measuring an organization's emissions of greenhouse gases, and can be viewed as an application of LCA. This topic is covered in some detail because of the importance of global warming in shaping businesses' strategies and the fact that many firms voluntarily disclose their carbon emissions. The third part of Chapter 4 focuses on environmental management systems and ISO 14001, a topic of importance given the increase in ISO 14001 adoption throughout the world, following a path similar to ISO 9000 in quality management systems. Finally, the last part of Chapter 4 discusses green building and LEED Certification. This was included given the exponential increase in

LEED Certifications, as shown in Chapter 4. Chapter 10 provides some fundamental concepts in renewable energy and biofuels, which are key to reducing an organization's carbon footprint.

Chapters 5–7 are focused on "closing the loop," the final step in the path of Figure 1.2. Chapter 5 covers DfE. The chapter starts by presenting several general guidelines adopted in many DfE design protocols (such as materials selection, reduced energy consumption, etc.). Considering that packaging corresponds to 30 percent of the municipal solid waste in the United States, and it is a key component of product design, the second part of Chapter 5 presents the idea of packaging scorecard, including an example. The chapter then presents general guidelines for design for remanufacturing (such as the need for modularity, design for disassembly, etc.). Finally, the chapter concludes with an overview of an important design protocol, cradle-to-cradle, which presents some novel conceptual ideas.

Chapter 6 is about servicizing (i.e., the idea of selling services as opposed to products) and leasing, which are business models that facilitate recovery of a product post-consumer use, and can thus support a CLSC structure. The first part of Chapter 6 discusses the environmental benefits and drawbacks of servicizing and leasing. Then, accounting aspects of leasing are discussed, including the differences between operating and capital leases. Finally, the chapter concludes by providing an actual spreadsheet example, which illustrates the financial implications of a firm considering whether to buy or lease.

Chapter 7 presents an overview of remanufacturing, starting with an introduction about the scope of remanufacturing in the United States and abroad. The chapter then discusses product acquisition and remarketing—two key characteristics that differentiate remanufacturing from regular manufacturing, considering that the main input to remanufacturing operations is product returns, post-consumer use. The chapter then concludes with an overview of remanufacturing practice in four select industries: automotive engines, cartridges, cell phones, and Internet networking equipment; the industries were selected to illustrate the diversity of practices across industries, as well as challenges.

Considering that firms operate in supply chains, Chapter 8 describes the idea behind environmental product differentiation,[9] which is a useful framework in understanding how triple bottom line firms select suppliers and source products. In particular, the chapter discusses different ecolabels, some of which establish credible information about the product's green (or ethical) attributes to customers. In addition, many ecolabels have chain of custody requirements, which necessitate a rethinking of how firms design their supply chains in certain cases (e.g., food and wood products).

1.6   Web Resources

Because sustainability is an evolving and dynamic field, Web links are provided at the end of each chapter when appropriate, which provide more in-depth information about a particular topic. In general, several websites are specialized in collecting and disseminating news on sustainability. For some, the reader can subscribe to obtain a daily summary sent to his/her inbox. These include:

- Environmental Leader: http://www.environmentalleader.com/
- Sustainable Business: http://www.sustainablebusiness.com/
- Ethical Corporation: http://www.ethicalcorp.com/

CHAPTER 2

Take-Back Legislation

2.1 Introduction

Traditionally, the handling of waste has been the responsibility of local governments and municipalities. In addition, during the past 60 years or so, the industrial paradigm for the manufacturing of consumer goods has been to design and manufacture products for a single life cycle: minimizing material use (so as to minimize cost), so that products are less expensive but have to be discarded upon failure or obsolescence, rather than being repaired. One could argue that the fast evolution in technology is a significant driver of this trend. In industrialized countries, it is often more expensive to repair an electronic product or appliance than to buy a new one. For consumer electronics, this is partly due to their shorter life cycles, a result of increased performance and lower cost associated with semiconductor manufacturing, that is, the fast learning curve of the industry. With the digital revolution, the evolution of the electronics industry is driven partly by the pace at which microprocessor and memory manufacturers can reduce the size of transistors, and as a result increase the number of transistors per circuit, allowing processing of more data, since one transistor is associated with one bit of memory. Moore's Law states that the number of transistors per chip doubles roughly every 18 months.

Shortening of life cycles and fast evolution of technology, however, result in an unfortunate by-product: the exponential increase in e-waste. The number of computers sold worldwide was 183 million in 2004, and 260 million in 2016.[1] Most municipalities are clearly not prepared to handle the processing of this exponential increase in e-waste, particularly because electronic products contain toxic substances (such as mercury, cadmium, lead, and others), and recycling of electronic products is for the most part unprofitable. As a result, legislators have been enacting product take-back legislation, based on the principle of Extended Producer Responsibility (EPR). EPR holds producers physically and financially responsible for collection and environmentally responsible treatment of their products at the end of their useful life. There exists, in numerous forms or jurisdictions, take-back legislation for packaging, automobiles, appliances, and e-waste. In this chapter, we focus mostly on take-back legislation for e-waste, due to its complexity, reach, and impact on producers and society in general.

Very broadly speaking, take-back legislation takes three basic forms:

1. Advanced recovery fee (ARF; *consumer pays*): here consumers are assessed a fee upon the purchase of a new product. Retailers collect the fee and pass it to government, who uses a significant portion of the fee to subsidize collectors and recyclers.

2. Unit-based fee (*consumer pays*): here, the fee is collected upon the disposal of a used product, as opposed to during the sale of a new product.

3. Collection and recycling targets (*producer pays*): here, producers must collect a specified amount of used products, and recycle a certain fraction of the collected products.

Although we have used the terms "producer pays" and "consumer pays," it is clear that both consumers and producers are likely to share costs for financing recycling of used products. In the ARF example, there are certain design guidelines established for producers to facilitate recycling; in the case of the unit-based fee, producers are still likely to be required to establish their own recycling networks, and in the case of collection and recycling targets, consumers are likely to experience higher prices for new products.

In the case of collection and recycling targets, a fair implementation of the legislation would ensure that each producer would be responsible solely for its own waste, that is, each producer would collect and recycle only its own products. This principle is referred to as *Individual Producer Responsibility* (IPR). In practice, IPR is difficult to achieve for the following reasons: recycling is subject to significant economies of scale, and e-waste transportation for long distances increases recycling costs. In addition, many collection points are set up by municipalities, so that all e-waste (across all products, manufacturers, and models) is collected together, resulting in a logistic nightmare for sorting. We provide some specific examples of take-back legislation in the following sections.

2.2   Take-Back Legislation in Electronics: Europe

The European Union (EU) established the WEEE Directive in 2003 to require producers to be financially and physically responsible for the recovery of e-waste. A recast of the WEEE Directive was approved by the EU parliament in February of 2012, with revised (more stringent) collection and recycling targets. The collection target was changed from a fixed amount (4 kg per year per inhabitant) to a collection *rate* target of 65 percent. According to the new directive[2]:

> From 2016, the minimum collection rate shall be 45 percent calculated on the basis of the total weight of WEEE collected in accordance with Articles 5 and 6 in a given year in the Member State concerned, expressed as a percentage of the average weight of EEE placed on the market in the three preceding years in that Member State.... From 2019, the minimum collection rate to be achieved annually shall be 65 percent of the average weight of EEE placed on the market in the three preceding years in the Member State concerned, or alternatively 85 percent of WEEE generated on the territory of that member state.

There are also recycling and recovery targets. *Recycling target* is the percentage (in weight) of the amount collected that is used for material recovery (i.e., recycling or reuse). *Recovery target* is the percentage (in weight) of the amount collected that is used for material and energy (i.e., incineration) recovery. The legislation stipulates different recycling and recovery targets for 11 product categories, and Table 2.1 illustrates the recycling targets for four product categories. So, for example, for large household appliances producers must recycle (or reuse) at least 80 percent of the amount of used products collected and allocated to the producer, and the total recovery target must exceed 85 percent; if a producer

Table 2.1 Illustration of recycling targets for WEEE directive

Category	Recycling target (%)	Recovery target (%)
Large household appliances	80	85
IT & telecommunications	70	80
Electric and electronic tools, medical equipment, monitoring devices, control equipment	55	75
Gas discharge lamps	85	85

recycles, say, 81 percent, then it must incinerate at least an additional 4 percent to meet the 85 percent recovery target. The directive has been transposed into national laws by each of the EU member state, and the way it has been implemented varies considerably across countries.

Table 2.2, adapted from Atasu and Van Wassenhove,[3] displays the differences in implementation of the directive between Germany (and the UK) and Belgium. In Belgium, municipalities and retailers collect e-waste. There is a single collective collection and recycling organization (CRO) (that is, a monopolist CRO, backed by industry and government), which all producers must use, and this CRO assesses producers a fee based on

Table 2.2 e-Waste take-back legislation in different countries in the EU

Dimension	Belgium	UK and Germany
Who performs collection	• Municipalities • Retailers	• Municipalities • Retailers • Producer's own collection system
Collection and recycling organizations (CRO)	• Single collective CRO	• Different competing collective CROs • Producer's own CRO allowed
Who pays for recycling costs	• Producers assessed recycling fees based on products sold • Consumers assessed an ARF	• Actual recycling costs split according to market share

Source: Adapted from Atasu and Van Wassenhove (2012).

the amount of products they sell (the fee is not necessarily correlated with actual recycling costs). In addition, consumers are also assessed an ARF. In the UK and Germany, there is no ARF assessed to consumers, and each producer is allowed to establish its own CRO, or form a collective CRO with other firms (for example, the European Recycling Platform, or ERP, is a CRO established by HP, Sony, Braun, and Electrolux). Finally, actual recycling costs (incurred by the CRO) are split among the different manufacturers according to market share.

2.3   Take-Back Legislation in Japan

The Specified Household Appliance Recycling (SHAR) law in Japan applies to TV sets, refrigerators, washing machines, and air conditioners; consumers are assessed a unit-based fee upon their disposal of the old appliance. This occurs when the consumer replaces an old appliance with a new one, so that the collection of old appliances occurs at retailers. The key to this system is an information system called the "manifest" system. Upon collecting an old appliance from a consumer, the retailer scans the barcode on the item. Each item (product category and brand) has associated with it on the manifest system a "recycling bill," which is a directive set forth by the producer indicating to the retailer to which CRO the used product should be sent. A CRO can be individually owned by a producer, or serve several producers (i.e., there are multiple competing CROs). If a CRO serves several producers, they are able to assess each producer the actual recycling cost for the producer's products (so, recycling costs are not split to producers based on, for example, market share as is the case in Germany). The manifest system also allows CROs to provide feedback to producers on ease of recyclability, for example, ease of disassembly, labeling, and material composition. The Japanese SHAR system is widely regarded as an example that approximates IPR, since manufacturers have control over their own recycling costs. Thus, the Japanese system provides an incentive for greener product designs.

Japan also has take-back legislation for personal computers (PCs). The differences from SHAR are: collection of used products is performed through the postal system, and consumers are not assessed a unit-based fee upon disposal.

2.4   Take-Back Legislation in the United States

As of May 2017, 25 states in the United States plus the District of Columbia have passed e-waste recycling laws.[4] The laws apply mostly to desktops, laptops, and monitors, with some laws also applying to printers and TVs. California is the only state in the U.S. where consumers pay an ARF: the money collected goes to the state, which uses it to reimburse recyclers and collectors. The other 24 states have producer responsibility take-back laws. The details vary across states. For example, in Virginia, Texas, and South Carolina (among others), the legislation only mandates financial producer responsibility for e-waste originating from consumers (but not businesses); in addition, there are no minimum collection and recycling targets. Due to inherent complexity and diversity of formats of the legislation in the different states, a comprehensive table that includes all 25 states is beyond the scope of this book; however, the reader is referred to a table that compares them.[5] For illustration, Table 2.3 displays examples of take-back legislation in three different states of the United States.

Table 2.3 indicates that in New York, Washington, and Indiana producers decide how they meet their recycling obligations: by owning their own recycling plants, contracting with other (private) collective CROs, or in the case of Washington, joining a collective state-operated CRO, with costs assessed based on return share (i.e., the actual volume of products recycled). The legislation also exempts producers from paying recycling costs for large businesses.

2.5   Implications for Producers and Policy Makers

Take-back legislation is a reality. In the United States, the dominant form of take-back legislation is that of producer responsibility, with the producer deciding how to meet recycling targets—that is, the producer decides which CRO to subcontract with. The exception is California, where consumers are assessed an ARF, with the money collected going to the state to reimburse collectors and recyclers. Japan also holds producers responsible for collection and recycling of appliances and PCs, although consumers pay a unit-based fee for appliances they dispose of. In Europe,

Table 2.3 Select examples of take-back legislation in the United States

Dimension	New York	Washington	Indiana
Who performs collection	• Municipalities • Producer's own collection system	• Municipalities • Retailers • Producer's own collection system	• Municipalities • Producer's own collection system
Collection and recycling organizations (CRO)	• Producer can own or subcontract with different CROs	• Producer can own, subcontract with different CROs, or join collective state-operated CRO	• Producer can own or subcontract with different CROs
Who pays for recycling costs	• Producers; recycling goals based on market share	• Producers • In the case of collective state CTO, cost allocated to producers according to return share	• Producers; recycling goals based on market share
Collection and recycling targets	• State-wide goal: Adjusted annually; 5 lbs/ person in 2013 • Producers assigned their own goal based on market share	• By convenience: manufacturers must have collection sites in every county plus every city of 10,000 or more	• 80% of amount sold
Who gets free recycling	• All except large businesses (>50 employees)	• Consumers, charities, schools, small businesses	• Consumers, public schools, small businesses (<100 employees)

some countries (such as Belgium and Sweden) have a monopolistic CRO, which producers must join, and producers are assessed recycling fees that do not necessarily reflect their actual recycling costs. In other countries, such as the UK, Germany, and France, producers also decide which CRO to use when meeting their recycling obligations, with their own recycling targets based on market share, from an overall collection target of 65 percent of sales.

The implication of these examples to producers is clear: producers who invest in recycling technologies (and easy-to-recycle products) will be able to meet their recycling obligations more cheaply (or even turn a profit from recycling) under several take-back laws that favor individual producer responsibility (several states in the United States, Japan, and many countries in Europe). In jurisdictions where the take-back is handled by a single collective system (monopolistic or state-run CROs), there is evidently no incentive for producers to invest in recycling technologies, or in greener products. However, even in these cases, proactive producers can still lobby governments to revise the implementation of these take-back laws so as to approximate IPR. Proactive and efficient producers prefer a level playing field where they are responsible only for their own waste so that efficient recycling technologies and greener (in the context of easy-to-recycle) products will be another source of competitive advantage, considering that lower recycling costs, and higher revenues from recycled material, will be passed on to consumers in the form of lower prices.

A recent development in e-waste recycling is that, for many electronic products, firms can now turn profits from recycling them. This is due to many reasons such as a sharp increase in the prices of precious metals (thus incentivizing recovery of such metals), advances in product design, and improvements in recycling technology. Although this is good news for producers who have to comply with recycling targets, this development also causes them a headache: because recycling can be profitable, some e-waste is leaked to third-party recyclers and/or exported to other countries. This may make it difficult for producers to comply with their recycling target obligations. In fact, many academics and practitioners have called for a refocus of take-back legislation from establishing recycling targets for producers toward stricter recycling standards to ensure that third-party recycling is done appropriately.

To policy makers, the implications are that society benefits from take-back laws that favor IPR: manufacturers will design greener products, recycling costs will decrease, and consumers will benefit from cheaper recycling costs in the form of low product prices. When designing new take-back legislation, or when revising existing legislation, policy makers can learn from Europe, countries such as Japan, and from some states in the United States. Implementation details, however, matter: producers should be allowed to design their own collection and recycling system.

2.6   Web Resources

Since the legislative environment on take-back legislation changes rapidly, the reader is referred to the following websites for constantly updated information:

- Take-back Legislation in the U.S.: http://www.electronicstake-back.com
- WEEE Directive in Europe: http://ec.europa.eu/environment /waste/weee/index_en.htm

CHAPTER 3

The First Step Toward Sustainability—Lean and Six-Sigma

3.1 The Lean Management Philosophy: Types of Waste

Lean and six-sigma are two mainstream process improvement methodologies. Several books have been written about these two methodologies; as a result, this chapter will only summarize some main points. Although some purists may not agree completely, "lean manufacturing," "Toyota Production System (TPS)," and "Big Just-in-Time" are three different names referring to the same thing. In a nutshell, the objective of lean is to reduce waste (*muda*, in Japanese) in all aspects of a firm's production activities: human relations, vendor relations, technology, and the management of materials and inventory. There are seven forms of waste:

1. *Overproduction.* This is waste from producing products and services when they are not immediately needed. Examples: production in large batches in manufacturing, and returning excess surgical supplies to the shelf in health care.
2. *Transportation.* This is waste from moving products or parts from one physical location to another. As an example, work-in-process (WIP) inventory is moved from one end of a manufacturing plant to the other end, as a result of the layout of the facility, that is, the location of manufacturing equipment within the facility.

3. *Inventory.* In lean, inventory is considered waste. Of course, a certain amount of inventory is necessary to protect against uncertainties inherent in processes, but lean views inventory as an impediment to the observation and correction of process problems. This is illustrated with the "rocks in the river" analogy in Figure 3.1. In this analogy, the water level represents WIP inventory, and the rocks represent problems in the process. By lowering the amount of inventory (through, for example, a *kanban* system, which we explain later), the firm is able to uncover problems in the production process. In Figure 3.1, for example, if inventory is lowered by a small amount, the firm will notice machine breakdowns (that is, inventory was high to protect against machine breakdowns). The firm then implements a preventive maintenance program. The firm continues to lower inventories, and then uncovers materials that are out of spec; the firm then works with suppliers to address that. And so forth.

4. *Waiting Time.* This is waste incurred when people (employees) wait for the arrival of some part, information, or equipment to accomplish a task. For example, when operators wait for parts to arrive from an upstream process step, or when doctors are waiting for lab results.

5. *Motion Waste.* This is similar to transportation waste, but here it is related to people. For example, when a machine operator walks 20 ft to another room to pick up a tool that is needed to setup a machine

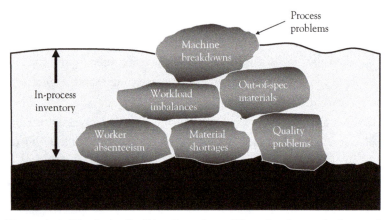

Figure 3.1 "Rocks in the River" analogy: Water level must be lowered.

for production. As another example, when a nurse has to take an elevator and go down two floors to pick up supplies to care for a patient.

6. *Processing Waste.* This is waste related to unnecessary process steps. For example, if there is too much paperwork, or when a patient is required to go through redundant or unnecessary steps because the doctor practices defensive medicine.

7. *Defects.* This is a natural definition of waste for most people—fixing defects. For example, rework (when a defect is caught in production before reaching the final customer), warranty claims, recalls, hospital infections.

The seven forms of waste are summarized in Figure 3.2.

Three Japanese words are frequently used to characterize the lean philosophy:

- *Heijunka.* This means, level the load by reducing workload imbalances between different steps of the production process, reducing setup times (and costs), and reducing variability within the process. All of these result in reduced inventories. We discuss

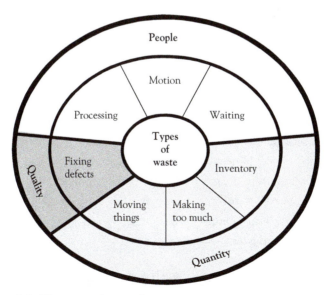

Figure 3.2 The seven forms of waste.

this in more detail later when we address pull production, one of the "tools" of lean.

- *Jidoka*. This means, stop the process immediately (sacrificing output) to address an immediate production problem. At Toyota manufacturing plants, there are *andon* cords that run parallel to the assembly line, and a worker can pull an *andon* cord at any time (if a defect or problem is found) to stop the production line. In auto manufacturing, stopping a production line is an expensive proposition, since a typical line manufactures one car every 90 seconds or so. Thus, the use of the *andon* cord provides strong incentives to find and fix defects where they occur.
- *Kaizen*. This means a relentless, long-term commitment to process and quality improvement.

3.2   Lean Toolkit

Pull Processes and Setup Time Reduction

The basic idea behind pull processes is to significantly reduce WIP in the system, and as a result, reduce throughput, or lead times (i.e., the total time a unit spends in the system, including waiting and processing). This is because inventories and throughput times are related through Little's Law:

$$\text{Average Throughput Time} = \frac{\text{Average WIP}}{\text{Production Rate}} \qquad 3.1$$

A consequence of Equation 3.1 is that there are only two ways to decrease throughput times:

- Increase the production rate. This most likely necessitates investments in equipment or labor, because the production rate of a process is equal to the rate of the bottleneck resource.
- Decrease WIP. This can be accomplished by using a "pull process," which sets the amount of WIP in the system to a constant value, as discussed later.

In a *push* process, work is *scheduled* and pushed through each stage in the process in order to meet specified delivery dates for finished products

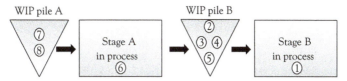

Figure 3.3 Illustration of push and pull processes in a two-stage process. (Each circle with a number represents one unit of WIP.)

and services. That is, work happens in anticipation of demand forecasts. Consider the simple two-stage process in Figure 3.3, where each circle with a number represents one unit of WIP. Stage A will deliver unit 6 to WIP Pile B as soon as it finishes its processing. In a push process, the upstream stage (stage A) authorizes the downstream stage (stage B) to work by delivering WIP.

On the other hand, in a *pull* process, work at each state in the production process is pulled through the system by actual demand for final products and services. One way to implement a pull process is through a *kanban* system *(kanban* means card in Japanese), where the WIP for each stage in the process is set to a constant (i.e., the amount of WIP at that stage is equal to the number of *kanbans* designed for it). This can be seen in Figure 3.3, where the size of the *kanban* at stage B is four units (that is, the maximum WIP waiting to start processing at stage B—WIP Pile B— is four units). If stage A completes its work on unit 6, it will only deliver that unit to WIP Pile B when stage B completes work on unit 1. At that time, unit 6 is delivered to WIP Pile B, and stage A can start working on unit 7. In a pull process, the downstream stage (stage B) authorizes the upstream stage (stage A) to work in order for WIP to be constant.

The size of the *kanban* (i.e., the amount of WIP the system is allowed to maintain) is related to the amount of variability in the system, including quality. A highly variable system with lower amounts of WIP results in frequent process stoppages. To see this, consider again Figure 3.3: if the throughput rate of stage B becomes higher than that of stage A, then it is possible that stage B will consume all the WIP in WIP Pile B before A is able to "catch up," which may result in an empty WIP Pile B; stage B will be starved and the process will stop. Lean is also concerned with removing variability and workload imbalances in the system, so that there is less idle time (or production stoppages) overall.

In addition, if stage B identifies quality issues with units 2–5 and these have to be re-sent to stage A for rework, then stage B again will be starved. That is why *jidoka* and *kaizen* are essential components of lean: without quality, it is not possible to implement a pull process effectively.

Setup time (cost) is a fixed time (cost) needed for an operation to take place, regardless of the quantity processed. As an example, consider the process of slicing cheeses at a deli, which requires positioning of the cheese at the machine and calibrating it for the required thickness before the slicing can begin, regardless of the number of slices processed. Setup times are not only common in manufacturing, but they also exist in services: consider the loss in productivity that result from a worker switching tasks. Setup times result in inventories, because operations need to be carried out in batches (so that the fixed setup time can "distributed" among more units), and as a result, units are processed in advance of when they are needed. Lean seeks to achieve small batches through the use of setup reduction techniques, such as SMED.[1] SMED typically starts by filming the setup process, and identifying possible ways to reduce the time involved in it, for example, positioning needed tools closer to the worker, or designing and using fixtures that make calibration less time consuming.

Value Stream Mapping

Value stream mapping can be thought of as a process flow chart where activities are identified as belonging to one of three types:

- Value Added activities (VA): activities in a process for which the customer is willing to pay. Examples include nursing care, surgery, or a worker assembling a wheel in a car production line.
- Non Value Added activities (NVA): activities for which the customer is not willing to pay, and are not necessary for business. Examples include a nurse walking 50 ft to another room to search for supplies, or a worker retrieving inventory from a warehouse.
- Business Non Value Added (BNVA): activities for which the customer is not willing to pay, but are necessary for accounting, legal, or regulatory purposes. Examples include preparing financial statements, or disclosing information to regulatory agencies.

In a value stream map, additional information is typically included in the chart displaying the activities. Examples include processing time per unit, wait time, estimated cost, and changeover cost. The objective of a value stream map is to reduce waste in the process by eliminating or reducing NVA activities. Figure 3.4 displays a value stream map for part of a process at an assembly plant. The only VA activity in Figure 3.4 is the assembly of the product by the technician, and that is shaded in gray. The other activities constitute waste. Moving parts around the plant constitute transportation waste. Inspection activities constitute processing waste (if there was an effective quality program in place, there would be no need for inspection). Storage constitutes inventory waste. For any value stream map, we define process efficiency as the percentage of time the process is spent in VA activities. For the process in Figure 3.4:

$$\text{Process efficiency} = \frac{\text{Time spent in value added activities}}{\text{Total process time (throughput time)}} \qquad 3.2$$

$$= \frac{13}{5 + 3 + 10 + 15 + 5 + 13 + 3} = 23$$

Efficiencies around 20 percent are common in batch manufacturing, where there is considerable waiting time. At some service organizations, efficiencies can be much higher. For example, at Virginia Mason Medical Center, a hospital in Seattle (WA), the process efficiency for breast cancer

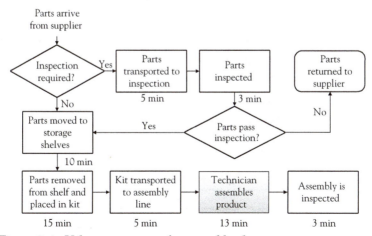

Figure 3.4 Value stream map for assembly plant.

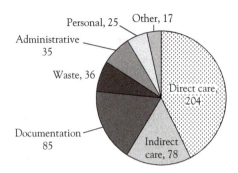

Figure 3.5 Value stream map for a nurse's time during an 8-hour shift (480 minutes).

diagnosis and treatment was reported to be 70 percent.[2] In fact, Figure 3.5 shows a value stream map for a nurse's time at an actual hospital in the mid-Atlantic area of the United States. It can be seen that VA activities constitute 282 minutes (204 + 78) out of the 480 minutes of the nurse's time, for an efficiency of 59 percent. BNVA activities constitute 120 minutes (85 + 35), or 25 percent. The 36 minutes of waste in this example comprise activities such as looking for equipment, looking for supplies, waiting delays, and others. Although 36 minutes of waste constitute only 7.5 percent of the total time of the nurse, improvements here can have an impact, considering one would have to multiply these numbers by the number of shifts and the number of nurses in the hospital.

5S

5S is a system of procedures that are used to organize and arrange the workplace, in order to optimize performance, cleanliness, and safety. The meaning of each of the 5Ss is displayed in Table 3.1.

Table 3.1 The meaning of each of the 5Ss

Japanese S	English S
Seiri	Sorting
Seiton	Simplifying access (or, Set in order)
Seiso	Sweeping (or, Shine)
Seiketsu	Standardization
Shitsuke	Self-Discipline (or, Sustain)

Before   After

Figure 3.6 Implementation of 5S at a tech support department.

Figure 3.6 shows a picture of a tech support department before and after 5S implementation. A typical 5S implementation can be accomplished through the following five steps[3]:

1. Plan a course of action: Obtain 5S materials, coordinate activities with all departments involved, select a team, and develop a schedule.
2. Educate the work group: This is key, so that workers in the department know the objectives, and what will be involved. Ideally, the work group should be involved in the 5S implementation, but that is not necessary—it could be done by another group responsible for productivity improvements.
3. Evaluate the work area: Map and photograph the area, define boundaries, and conduct 5S appraisals (see Table 3.2).
4. Initiate the 5S: Sort unnecessary items (e.g., use red tags, use it or lose it auctions), simplify access, sweep, etc.
5. Measure results and maintain the workplace neat (this is the last S).

Layout Redesign

The idea behind layout redesign is to reduce transportation and motion waste. Traditionally, work areas have been designed around functional layouts, where each physical location of a facility is dedicated to a particular type of equipment—that is, each physical location in the facility performs a particular function. Figure 3.7 illustrates a typical functional layout in a manufacturing plant, with five different functions (saw, grinder, lathe, press, and heat treat areas), and each function confined to a single different area in the layout. The flow lines represent the flow of a typical

Table 3.2 Example of a 5S appraisal sheet

Sorting	Yes	No
1. Do all teams know this program is in place?		
2. Have criteria been defined to distinguish between necessary and unnecessary items?		
3. Have all unnecessary items been removed from the area?		
Simplifying access		
4. Is there a visually marked, specified place for everything?		
5. Is everything in its specified place?		
Sweeping		
6. Are work and break areas, offices, and rooms clean and orderly?		
7. Are cleaning guidelines and schedules visible?		
Standardizing		
8. Are current processes documented?		

Source: Peterson and Smith (1998).

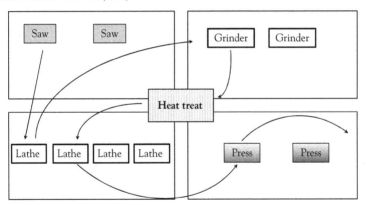

Figure 3.7 A typical functional layout.

product in that layout: saw → lathe → grinder → heat treat → lathe → press. Note how the product moves significantly across different physical areas of the plant, which indicates a considerable amount of transportation and motion waste.

Suppose now that the layout is then redesigned as a cellular layout, and that is shown in Figure 3.8. That layout has two cells: A and B, with the only heat treatment station being shared between cells A and B. This new layout minimizes transportation and motion waste, as the typical travel

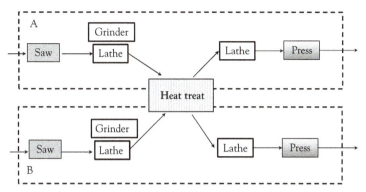

Figure 3.8 *Reorganization of layout from **Figure 3.7** into a cellular layout.*

time of a product in the facility is shortened considerably. The drawback from the cellular layout is the loss of "pooling" among identical machines. For example, suppose that in Figure 3.8 the firm produces two products, A and B, where product type A is processed in cell A, and product type B is processed in cell B. If the saw in cell A is busy and the saw in cell B is idle, then a product of type A will have to wait until the saw in cell A becomes available. This is despite the fact that the other saw (in cell B) is available, because cell B only processes products of type B. This situation would not arise in the functional layout of Figure 3.7. In most applications, however, a typical manufacturing plant processes multiple (sometimes hundreds) of product types, and production cells are designed so that a cell works on a *family* of products that share *similar* processing requirements.

Although the examples in Figures 3.7 and 3.8 are from a manufacturing environment, the idea of cellular layouts can certainly be applied to services. Examples in a hospital environment include: (i) creating self-contained administrative units, (iii) providing data entering devices for nurses and doctors located near patients (as opposed to only in offices), (iv) optimizing patient flow, and (iv) optimizing staff flow through reconfiguration of work stations.

3.3   Six-Sigma: Similarities and Differences with Lean

Six-sigma is another process improvement methodology that is focused in *reducing variation in processes,* and it can be summarized on the DMAIC

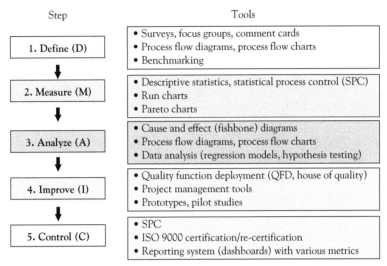

Step	Tools
1. Define (D)	• Surveys, focus groups, comment cards • Process flow diagrams, process flow charts • Benchmarking
2. Measure (M)	• Descriptive statistics, statistical process control (SPC) • Run charts • Pareto charts
3. Analyze (A)	• Cause and effect (fishbone) diagrams • Process flow diagrams, process flow charts • Data analysis (regression models, hypothesis testing)
4. Improve (I)	• Quality function deployment (QFD, house of quality) • Project management tools • Prototypes, pilot studies
5. Control (C)	• SPC • ISO 9000 certification/re-certification • Reporting system (dashboards) with various metrics

Figure 3.9 Six-sigma's DMAIC process and some tools that can be used in each step.

steps as shown in Figure 3.9. As can be seen, six-sigma is heavily focused on decision-making using data and statistical tools, which clearly demand a significant amount of training. In addition to tools, six-sigma is very disciplined, and involves full-time personnel with full knowledge of all the tools (*black belts*), as well as workers with a good knowledge of the tools, who work on these initiatives part time (perhaps 10–20 hours a week; the *green belts*). A black belt may have 4–6 weeks of training in the methodology plus experience in implementing it in actual projects. A green belt may have 25 hours of training in the methodology.

Six-sigma and lean are both focused on continuous, incremental improvement of existing processes, as opposed to radical redesign. Some of the tools are common, such as the use of process flow charts, run charts, and data collection. The tools in lean, as seen before, are more straightforward and do not require extensive statistical training as is the case with six-sigma. The two are complementary in that reducing variation in processes reduces the amount of waste. This is shown in Figure 3.10, where the "bell shape" curve represents the histogram of measurements for a particular variable of interest x (say, weight of a can of tuna), $\bar{x}$, σ_A and σ_B represent the average value, standard deviation of the value for process A, and standard deviation of the value for process B for that variable. With

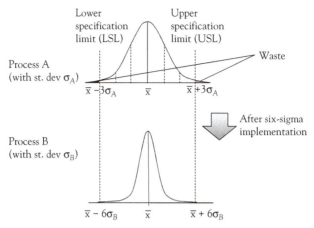

Figure 3.10 *Relationship between variability reduction and waste reduction.*

six-sigma implementation, the variability in the process is reduced ($\sigma_B <$ σ_A) and as a result fewer units fall outside the engineering specification limits.

3.4   Why is Lean Green?

Lean is green because waste reduction is associated with lower resource consumption, whether in the form of energy or raw materials; in addition, solid waste is reduced. For example, the Wausau Equipment Company, which produces machinery and equipment for the agribusiness industry, implemented lean at one of its plants and observed the following results[4]:

- Parts reworked decreased by 70 percent: this clearly reduces overall energy consumption, materials use, and solid waste.
- Throughput (production per unit time) increased by 35 percent: this represents a productivity improvement, which reduces overall energy consumption, and solid waste.

Thus, being lean is a first step toward being green.

CHAPTER 4

Eco-Efficiency and Metrics

4.1 Life-Cycle Assessment (LCA)

After lean implementation, the firm continues on its journey toward sustainability by moving toward eco-efficiency: reducing the environmental impact of products and processes. The first step in eco-efficiency is to have an understanding of the environmental impact of the firm's products and processes, and this is accomplished through life-cycle assessment (LCA). The objective of LCA is to find the full range of environmental (and sometimes, societal) damages assignable to products or processes through their entire life cycle, which comprises raw material extraction and processing, transportation, manufacturing, packaging and distribution, use by consumers, and end-of-life/disposal. Common categories of assessed damages include, but are not limited to: energy consumption, depletion of minerals and fossil fuels, global warming, toxicity (air, water, land, humans, and animals), ozone layer depletion, and acid rain. LCA is a data-intensive process, which is helped by the use of existing databases and software.

ISO14040, 14041, 14042, and 14043 provide guidelines for conducting an LCA, which is shown in Figure 4.1. The four steps are described now.

Goal and Scope Definition

In this step, the analyst must determine the **level of specificity** of the study: is the product or process analyzed specific to the firm or a particular manufacturing plant? For example, two different plants producing the same product could have different emission levels—one plant could have more modern, energy-efficient, and less polluting equipment than the other. An LCA specific to a product produced at a particular plant may

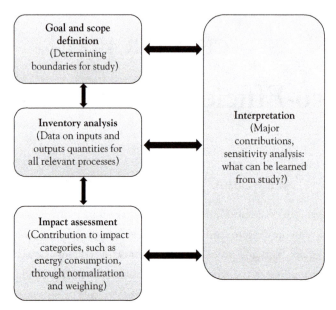

Figure 4.1 LCA phases (ISO 14040, ISO 14041, and 14044).

require an additional level of data collection that may be impractical and costly, and thus one may prefer to use industrial averages (for example, the impact of using aluminum as opposed to steel in a particular design), which are widely available, as we will see in some examples later. Related to this, the analyst will also need to determine the **level of accuracy** to be used in data collection and analysis. For internal decision-making in a firm (e.g., should we use product design A or B?), a reasonable estimate of environmental impacts is generally enough. If the study is used for driving public policy (e.g., should the government provide tax breaks for specific clean technologies?), however, a higher level of accuracy is desired.

Finally, if the goal of the study is to compare two alternative products, then the basis of comparison should be in terms of **equivalent use**. For example, if one is comparing bar soap versus liquid soap, then the basis of comparison should be the environmental impact (e.g., energy use) of manufacturing and using the products necessary for a given number of hand washings (say, 100 hand washings). As another example, if one is comparing fluorescent lights versus light emitting diodes (LED) lights, then the basis of comparison should be a given number of lighting hours: if one LED light lasts 25,000 hours and an incandescent light lasts 1,000 hours, then one should compare the environmental impact of manufacturing and using 1 LED light against 25 incandescent lights.

Regarding scope, the analyst must determine **which environmental concerns** should be addressed in the study (e.g., energy use, materials choice, solid waste, global warming potential, eutrophication, etc.). The analyst must also determine which stages of the life cycle will be addressed. In a **cradle-to-gate** LCA, only raw material extraction, transportation, manufacturing, and packaging and distribution are included, whereas in a **cradle-to-grave** LCA, use by consumers and end-of-life/disposal are also included (in addition to cradle-to-gate stages). This is shown in Figure 4.2.

Inventory Analysis and Impact Assessment

In this stage, the analyst collects data on the impacts of inputs and outputs generated by each life cycle stage on the assessed category of interest. There are databases available for common materials and processes used, which are industrial averages, and software is also widely available,

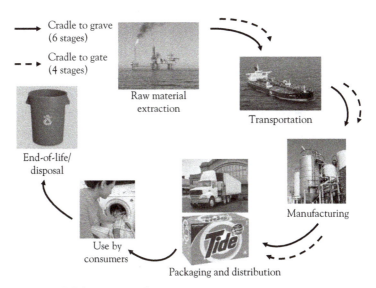

Figure 4.2 LCA stages and scope.

Table 4.1 Example of Product Assessment Matrix for LCA

Life cycle stage	Environmental concern	
	Materials choice	Energy use
Raw material extraction		
Transportation		
Manufacturing		
Packaging and distribution		
Use by consumers		
End-of-life/ disposal		

containing these databases. The site http://www.aclca.org contains some resources; different software providers include GaBi, SimaPro, and open-LCA. To illustrate, suppose the analyst has determined the scope of an LCA for a product to be of cradle-to-grave type, with two environmental concerns: materials choice and energy use. This is shown in Table 4.1. The analyst must now provide an assessment of how the product impacts the environment (regarding the choice of materials used in the design, as well as the energy use) for each of the six different life cycle stages. The assessment can be made using the actual number (for example, on energy consumption, GJ/ unit, or kWh), or on a scale (e.g., from 0 to 4, where 0 represents "no concern," and 4 represents "high concern").

Regarding materials choice, a good design would use materials with ample supply on earth, low rates of depletion, high potential for recycling, and low toxicity. Under these criteria, recommended materials may include aluminum, iron, carbon, hydrogen, manganese, nitrogen, oxygen, silicon, and titanium. Using the same criteria, the designer should avoid silver, gold, arsenic, cadmium, chlorine, chromium, mercury, nickel, and lead.

Regarding energy use, Table 4.2 contains some industrial averages for the amount of energy used to produce various metals. Notice how recycled materials consume a significantly lower amount of energy compared with primary production, particularly for aluminum, whose primary production is very energy intensive. As a result, assumptions about the percentage of recycled content on an aluminum part, for example, may make a significant impact on the final results of the LCA.

Table 4.2 Energy Use (GJ/mg) in Production of Various Metals[1]

Metal	Primary production	Secondary production (through recycling)
Steel	31	9
Copper	91	13
Aluminum	270	17
Zinc	61	24
Lead	39	9
Titanium	430	140

Examples

Table 4.3 compares paper versus plastic bags for use in grocery stores. The study addresses five different categories of environmental impact: materials choice, embodied energy, solid waste, total emissions to air, and global warming equivalents (in terms of CO_2 equivalents; we discuss later in this chapter the precise meaning of this term). The study compares the environmental impact of one paper bag against two plastic bags, as they both have similar carrying capacity. The study assumes current average recycling rates for paper and plastic in the United States. Table 4.3 indicates that paper bags have lower environmental impact in the categories of materials choice, and global warming potential. Plastic bags have lower environmental impact in the categories of solid waste, and total emissions to air; the two products have similar embodied energy (i.e., the energy necessary for manufacturing).

Figure 4.3 illustrates the global warming potential of desktop PCs and switching equipment conducted by NEC (the Japanese manufacturer). The

Table 4.3 Example of LCA: Paper versus Plastic Bag

Category of impact	Paper bag	Plastic bag
Materials choice	Wood (renewable)	Oil (nonrenewable)
Embodied energy (mJ)	1.7	1.5
Solid waste (in g)	50	14
Total emissions to air (kg)	2.6	1.1
Global warming potential (kg CO_2 equivalents)	0.23	0.53

Source: Institute for Lifecycle Energy Analysis.

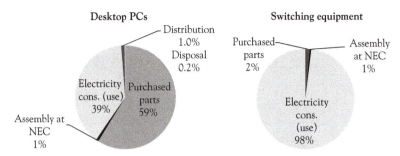

Figure 4.3 LCA (Global Warming) for different electronic products.
(Source: www.nec.com)

single assessed category of environmental impact is global warming potential (which is also called carbon footprint, as we will see later in this chapter), and the figure simply illustrates which stage of the product's life cycle contributes the most to global warming potential. The stages of the life cycle include purchased parts—the amount of global warming emissions related to manufacturing parts (including raw materials extraction) used in the products, final assembly at NEC, use by customers, distribution, and disposal. We first note that global warming potential is highly correlated to energy use, and emissions in the stage "use by customers" are related to global warming emissions associated with electricity production. For desktop PCs, most of the global warming potential (59 percent) is embodied in purchased parts, that is, during manufacturing of PC components, whereas use by customers represents 39 percent. Thus, reuse of desktops (through remanufacturing) is good for the environment, because reusing components (as opposed to manufacturing them from scratch) saves a significant amount of energy. With switching equipment, the vast majority of global warming emissions occur during use by customers (almost 98 percent), whereas purchased parts represent a little less than 2 percent. Thus, the remanufacturing of old, energy-inefficient switches is not good for the environment, unless remanufacturing is able to upgrade the product to newer, energy-efficient standards. For both products, product assembly at NEC represents about 1 percent of the global warming potential. The contribution of end-of-life and disposal is negligible for both products.

Figure 4.4 shows the results of an LCA performed by Osram and Siemens comparing three different alternatives for light bulbs:

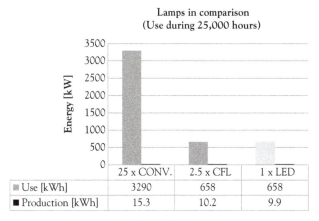

Figure 4.4 LCA of different light bulbs: conventional incandescent (CONV.), compact fluorescent (CFL), and LED. (Source: www .osram-os.com)

conventional incandescent bulbs, compact fluorescent lights (CFL), and LED lamps. The environmental impact assessed in Figure 4.4 is energy consumption during manufacturing and 25,000 hours of use by consumers. Traditional incandescent, CFL, and LED bulbs last on average 1,000, 10,000, and 25,000 hours, respectively. Thus, the appropriate comparison is energy usage for 25, 2.5, and 1 for incandescent, CFL, and LED bulbs, respectively, for both manufacturing and use with consumers. Just as in switching equipment, the stage "use by consumers" dominates the environmental impact of light bulbs; thus, the significant savings provided by CFL and LED bulbs. Although not shown here, the same study also analyzed human toxicity potential, global warming potential, and eutrophication as other environmental impact factors, and concluded that CFL and LED bulbs are again better than incandescent bulbs.

Limitations of LCA

Just like any other tool, LCA has its limitations:

1. Weights given to different impacts: The answer to an LCA is not always clear, particularly when the study is performed for multiple impacts, such as the paper versus plastic bag in Table 4.3. If the

analyst gives different weights to different impacts to come up with a single answer, then the weights are subjective.

2. Drawing the boundaries: Ideally, LCA studies should consider the entire environmental impact of a product through its life cycle, as in cradle-to-grave shown in Figure 4.2. Data can be easily collected by a firm to estimate environmental impact in the stages directly under its control, such as production, transportation, distribution, and packaging. Other stages (such as end-of-life and disposal) require assumptions such as existing recycling rates (which differ across locations), average hours of use, and so forth.

3. Social impacts: Environmental impacts are relatively easy to measure, but socio-economic impacts (such as well-being of impacted communities) are more difficult to quantify. A new framework for conducting social life cycle assessment has been developed by the United Nations Environmental Programme (UNEP). It considers five stakeholder categories: workers, local community, society, consumers, and value chain actors. Within each stakeholder category, there are impact categories as follows: human rights, working conditions, health and safety, cultural heritage, governance, and socio-economic conditions.

4. Renewable versus nonrenewable resources: An LCA that only considers energy consumption as an impact factor may fail to detect important issues with depletion of nonrenewable resources. Thus, materials choice (as an environmental impact factor) should be incorporated as often as possible.

In the next section, we provide a more in-depth discussion of a particular application of LCA: measuring a firm, product or process carbon footprint.

4.2   Measuring Carbon Footprint

Carbon footprint means the amount of greenhouse emissions associated with an organization (say, a firm), a product, or a process over a defined period of time. Carbon footprinting can be thought of as an application of LCA to the case where the environmental impact factor is global warming potential. The name "greenhouse gas" (GHG) refers to the manner in which certain gases—water vapor, methane (CH_4), carbon dioxide (CO_2), ozone (O_3), nitrous oxide (N_2O), hydrofluorocarbons (HFCs), and others—trap the energy generated by the sun in the earth, warming the planet. The presence of these gases in the atmosphere allows life as we know it to exist, and without them the planet would be significantly cooler. Due to different concentrations of these gases in the atmosphere, water vapor accounts for 36–70 percent of the greenhouse effect, carbon dioxide accounts for 9–26 percent, methane accounts for 4–9 percent, and ozone accounts for 3–7 percent. Industrial and human activities in general, however, are significant emitters of CO_2 and methane; the concentration of these two gases has increased by 40 percent and 125 percent, respectively, since 1850.[2]

Due to the warming potential of GHGs, firms have started tracking and reducing their emissions of these gases, even without government regulation. Because CO_2 is the most prevalent among the GHGs, it has become a standard for reporting all emissions of GHGs. Thus, firms report their total emissions of GHGs in terms of CO_2-equivalent, using conversion factors shown later in this chapter.

An **offset** is a compensatory measure made by a firm for its carbon emissions; this is usually done through financial support of projects (elsewhere, not inside the firm) that lower CO_2 emissions. A firm can reduce its own emissions by, for example, switching to a cleaner technology—for example, using solar panels to produce electricity for its retail stores, which Walmart has been doing—this is not an offset, but a direct reduction in Walmart's direct emissions. Alternatively, the firm can also sponsor the planting of trees in deforested areas (trees absorb CO_2), or provide financial support for a wind farm; those are examples of offsets—even though the firm's actual level of emissions may not have changed, net emissions in the planet are lowered by the trees it planted, or by the electricity produced via wind farms (which avoids consumption of coal).

In a **cap-and-trade** regulation, the government sets a "cap" on the amount of emissions allowed per year. After setting the cap, the government issues *allowances* to firms in certain industrial sectors—those that are heavy CO_2 emitters, such as utilities, paper, steel, and cement manufacturers—that gives these firms the right to emit a given quantity of GHGs in a year. Allowances may be auctioned, or allocated for "free."

A firm with annual emissions below its allowance can sell the difference (between its allowances and actual emissions) in the market, so that firms with emissions above their allowances can buy them. This system provides an economic incentive for firms to decrease their level of greenhouse emissions, because the government lowers the cap every year. Cap-and-trade has been used successfully to decrease the amount of SO_2 (which causes acid rain) in the atmosphere in the United States, that is, actual SO_2 emissions decreased over time since the program's implementation in 1995. Cap-and-trade for GHG is in Effect in the European Union since 2005; in the United States, there is no legislation at the federal level, although California passed its own legislation in October of 2011.

An alternative type of legislation aimed at reducing greenhouse emissions is a **carbon tax**, which is a tax levied on carbon emissions. A carbon tax could impose a tax on direct CO_2 emissions (say, $12 per ton of CO_2 emitted, which is abbreviated as $12/tCO_2$), or an energy tax, which is levied on the carbon content of fuels used (say, $43 per ton of carbon, abbreviated as $43/tCo_2$). British Columbia implemented a $10/tCO_2$ legislation in 2008, with the tax level increased later; it was $30/tCO_2$ in 2017.

The GHG protocol provides internationally recognized standards for firms to track their GHG emissions—corporate GHG accounting—and we discuss this next.

An Organization's Carbon Footprint

The GHG Protocol Corporate Standard[3] provides guidance for firms and other organizations to compute their GHG emissions. It covers the accounting and reporting of six GHGs: CO_2, methane (CH_4), nitrous oxide (N_2O), hydrofluorocarbons (HFCs), perfluorocarbons (PFCs), and sulfur hexafluoride (SF_6). The GHG protocol is a partnership between the World Business Council for Sustainable Development and the World Resources Institute. The CDP (formerly, Carbon Disclosure Project) is an organization (and data repository) that allows firms, cities, states, and countries to voluntarily disclose their carbon emissions, in order to track their progress toward emissions reductions, and to increase transparency of their operations.

To measure an organization's carbon footprint, the first step is to **set the boundaries** of the organization. Some organizations are complex entities: they may participate in joint ventures, subcontract some portion of their operations, and lease some assets. The GHG protocol recommends reporting at the highest level possible (say, the parent company, such as General Electric). For operations that are jointly owned, the GHG protocol suggests an equity share approach (where the organization reports emissions from wholly owned facilities, and a share corresponding to its equity share for partially owned facilities). Alternatively, the organization may decide to report all emissions from facilities that are under the organization's control, including both wholly and partially owned.

After setting the boundaries, the GHG protocol identifies three separate scopes for emissions:

1. *Scope 1.* These are emissions from the organization's own on-site operations: fossil fuel combustion in the organization's fleet vehicles (mobile combustion of fuels), fossil fuel combustion in local electricity production (stationary combustion of fuels), as well as gases generated by some manufacturing processes.
2. *Scope 2.* These are emissions resulting from the production of electricity purchased by the organization.
3. *Scope 3:* These include all upstream activities (extraction of raw materials, production of parts purchased by the firm, and transportation of these parts to the organization), downstream activities (distribution of the organization's products to distribution centers, and retailers, as well as product disposal), and travel and commuting by employees. Referring back to Figure 4.2, one can view Scope 1 emissions as related to the "manufacturing" portion of the product's life cycle, Scope 2 emissions as all the electricity purchased by the organization, and Scope 3 emissions as all the other stages in the cradle-to-grave LCA approach (except use by customers), in addition to employee travel and commuting. Notice that scope 3 for an organization is scope 1 or 2 for another organization.

Scope 1 and 2 emissions are relatively easy to compute, whereas Scope 3 emissions are much more complex. We notice, however, that for several firms and/or industries, the bulk of emissions are likely to be Scope 3, rather than Scopes 1 and 2. One study finds that Scopes 1 and 2 combined account for 26 percent, on average, of an industry's emissions.[4] Walmart states that "90 percent of our environmental impact exists beyond the footprint of our stores and facilities".[5] Due to the simplicity in calculation, and the fact that carbon legislation does not address Scope 3 emissions, however, we provide here an example of how to compute Scopes 1 and 2 emissions for a small firm. The reader is referred to the GHG protocol website (www.ghgprotocol.org) for guidelines on computing Scope 3 emissions.

Since there are multiple GHGs involved in the computation, all of their emissions are converted to CO_2 emissions, with the use of a global warming potential conversion factor. That is, the global warming potential of CO_2 is normalized to one. The global warming potential of the three main GHGs is shown in Table 4.4. From Table 4.4, 1 kg of CH_4 is equivalent to 25 kg of CO_2.

The next source of data concerns the emissions amount for common processes. For Scope 1 emissions, Table 4.5 presents emissions for the three

Table 4.4 Global warming potential of three main GHGs

GHG	Global warming potential
CO_2	1
CH_4	25
N_2O	298

Source: U.S. EPA.[6]

Table 4.5 Emissions Factor for Stationary Combustion of Fossil Fuels

Fossil fuel	kg CO_2/ MMBtu	kg CH_4/ MMBtu	kg N_2O/ MMBtu
Bituminous coal	93.46	0.0110	0.0016
Natural gas	53.06	0.0050	0.0001
Wood	93.87	0.3160	0.0042
Propane, LPG	63.07	0.0011	0.0006
Diesel, gasoline, kerosene	73.15	0.0110	0.0006

Source: U.S. EPA.[7]

Table 4.6 Emissions factors for mobile combustion of fossil fuels

Fossil fuel	kg CO_2/ gallon	kg CH_4/ gallon	kg N_2O/ gallon
Gasoline	8.81	0.0005	0.00022
Diesel	10.15	0.0006	0.00026
Ethanol	5.56	0.000042	0.000034

Source: U.S. EPA.[8]

main GHGs in the stationary combustion of fossil fuels, and Table 4.6 presents emissions for mobile combustion of fossil fuels.

For Scope 2 emissions, the emissions factors depend on where the electricity is purchased, since the amount of emissions (say, per MWh of electricity purchased) depends on how the electricity is produced, and different regions of the United States and the world generate electricity using a different mix of sources (coal, natural gas, nuclear, hydroelectric, wind, etc.). In the United States, the grid is divided into 26 sub-regions, as shown in Figure 4.5. The emissions factors for each of the 26 sub-regions, in terms of kilograms of each of the three gases per MWh of electricity purchased, are shown in Table 4.7.

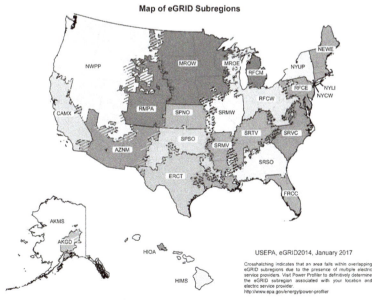

Figure 4.5 Sub-regions of the U.S. electricity grid. (Source: U.S. EPA)[9]

Table 4.7 Emissions factors for electricity purchased in different regions of the united states

Acronym	Sub-region name	kg CO_2/ MWh	kg CH_4/ MWh	kg N_2O/ MWh
AKGD	ASCC Alaska Grid	420.3	0.021	0.0032
AKMS	ASCC Miscellaneous	308.7	0.016	0.0027
AZNM	WECC Southwest	397.2	0.030	0.0042
CAMX	WECC California	257.9	0.015	0.0018
ERCT	ERCOT All	518.3	0.037	0.0053
FRCC	FRCC All	487.7	0.040	0.0055
HIMS	HICC Miscellaneous	426.7	0.043	0.0069
HIOA	HICC Oahu	671.1	0.072	0.0111
MROE	MRO East	754.7	0.087	0.0128
MROW	MRO West	619.2	0.073	0.0106
NEWE	NPCC New England	258.9	0.044	0.0058
NWPP	WECC Northwest	411.4	0.044	0.0065
NYCW	NPCC NYC/ Westchester	301.9	0.011	0.0013
NYLI	NPCC Long Island	542.6	0.060	0.0078
NYUP	NPCC Upstate NY	165.9	0.014	0.0019
RFCE	RFC East	376.2	0.034	0.0051
RFCM	RFC Michigan	694.7	0.077	0.0111
RFCW	RFC West	626.4	0.068	0.0100
RMPA	WECC Rockies	788.2	0.081	0.0117
SPNO	SPP North	714.4	0.079	0.0114
SPSO	SPP South	669.4	0.061	0.0089
SRMV	SERC Mississippi Valley	463.6	0.036	0.0051
SRMW	SERC Midwest	803.8	0.095	0.0138
SRSO	SERC South	518.8	0.047	0.0070
SRTV	SERC Tennessee Valley	606.1	0.063	0.0092
SRVC	SERC Virginia/ Carolina	388.5	0.043	0.0062
US	United States	509.3	0.050	0.0073

Source: U.S. EPA.[10]

Now, we show how to use the data provided above to estimate the carbon footprint of a landscaping business in North Florida. The firm has two pick-up trucks, and several gasoline-powered machines, such as mowers, trimmers, blowers, and so forth. The firm also owns a generator, which it occasionally uses to generate electricity for its office during power outages. Every year, the firm purchases about 6,800 gallons of gasoline for its two trucks and machines, about 2,500 MMBtus of natural gas for heating the offices and for the generator, and 10,000 kWh of electricity (that is equal to 10 MWh of electricity). The emissions are calculated as follows:

- Scope 1, natural gas (stationary): From Table 4.5, the emissions factors for CO_2, CH_4, and N_2O are 53.06, 0.005, and 0.0001 kg of gas per MMBtu, respectively. Since the firm consumes 2,500 MMBtu of natural gas per year, the corresponding emissions are 132,650 kg of CO_2, 12.5 (0.005 * 2,500) kg of CH_4, and 0.25 (0.0001* 2,500) kg of N_2O.

- Scope 1, gasoline (mobile): From Table 4.6, the emissions factors for CO_2, CH_4, and N_2O are 8.81, 0.0005, and 0.00022 kg of gas per gallon, respectively. Since the firm consumes 6,800 gallons of gasoline per year, then the corresponding emissions are 59,908 kg of CO_2, 3.4 kg of CH_4, and 1.5 kg of N_2O.

- Scope 2, electricity (grid): From Figure 4.5, the corresponding sub region for Florida is FRCC. From Table 4.7, the corresponding emissions factors for CO_2, CH_4, and N_2O are 487.7, 0.040, and 0.0055 kg of gas per MWh of electricity purchased, respectively. Since the firm consumes 10 MWh, the corresponding emissions are 4,877 kg of CO_2, 0.40 kg of CH_4, and 0.055 kg of N_2O.

Adding all emissions from Scope 1 and Scope 2 sources, we obtain 197,435 kg of CO_2, 16.3 kg of CH_4, and 1.8 kg of N_2O. From Table 4.4, the associated global warming factors are 1, 25 and 298 for CO_2, CH_4 and N_2O, respectively. Thus, the emissions in term of kilograms of CO_2 equivalent are 197,435 kg, 407 kg (16.3×25), and 537 kg (1.8×298) for CO_2, CH_4, and N_2O, respectively, for a grand total of 198,379 kg of CO_2 equivalent per year. Thus, the firm's carbon footprint is 198.4 tons of CO_2 equivalent per year. For ease of reference, the calculations are summarized in Table 4.8.

The U.S. EPA provides a tool for computing a household's own carbon footprint; this tool is available at: https://www3.epa.gov/carbon-footprint-calculator/.

Table 4.8 Summary of carbon footprint calculations for landscaping business example

Type	Sub type	Consumption	Factor CO_2	Factor CH_4	Factor N2O	kg CO_2	kg CH_4	kg N_2O
Gasoline	Mobile	6,800 gallons	8.81	0.0005	0.00022	59,908	3.40	1.5
Natural gas	Stationary	2,500 MMBtu	53.06	0.005	0.0001	132,650	12.50	0.250
Electricity	grid	10 MWh	487.7	0.040	0.0055	4,877	0.40	0.055
			Total			197,435	16.3	1.8
			Global Warming Potential			1	25	298
			Total kg CO_2 equivalent			197,435	407	537

A Product's Carbon Footprint

The previous section detailed a method to compute the carbon footprint for an organization as a whole. We can also compute the carbon footprint of a product, which is in essence a cradle-to-grave LCA with greenhouse emissions as the sole environmental impact factor. An example was discussed previously, in Figure 4.3, for NEC products, where the stage "use by customers" dominated switching equipment's carbon footprint due to the amount of electricity consumed by this product, which operates 24/7 for several years.

Notice that the reporting of a product's carbon footprint is entirely voluntary (whereas an organization's carbon footprint might be required by carbon legislation). There are standards for computing a product's carbon footprint, such as the PAS 2050 (released by the British Standard Institute), and the GHG Protocol, which was released in late 2011. The PAS 2050 standard has links to the ISO 14040 and ISO 14064 standards, which are also for carbon footprint (ISO standards are focused on requirements, as opposed to specific guidelines). The PAS standard is used by the Carbon Trust,[11] which is a nonprofit established by the UK government, with support from firms, to help firms measure carbon footprint, as well as implement low carbon technologies. Firms can also pursue Certification of their products from Carbon Trust, which allows them to use a label.

LCA and carbon footprint are metrics that identify a firm's environmental impact, for the organization as a whole, or for specific products and/or processes. The next step for the firm is to *improve* its environmental performance, and our next section discusses a process for this.

4.3   Environmental Management Systems and ISO 14001

An environmental management system (EMS) is a *process* designed to help a firm meet environmental objectives, mandated or not by legislation, and thus demonstrate improved environmental performance. The process described in an EMS is based on the plan-do-check-act (PDCA), or Deming's cycle, which is used in most quality management systems. Using a process based on quality management techniques is a natural fit, as one can think of environmental performance as a dimension of overall quality for the firm.

Depending on the scope of the firm's environmental activities, an EMS can be informal, with limited documentation, or a formal process, fully documented, particularly for firms exposed to significant environmental risks (say, in chemical manufacturing, or oil extraction and refining). Most firms that are subject to environmental legislation have an EMS designed exclusively for compliance with existing legislation. However, an EMS can be proactive, and designed to take a firm beyond compliance.

An EMS is likely to include clear procedures and documentation to deal with the following issues:

- *Do you have an environmental policy?* An environmental policy details the firm's approach to dealing with environmental issues. For example, an environmental policy may be very narrowly focused toward compliance with existing environmental legislation, or it may be very far reaching (e.g., the firm's goal is to be carbon neutral, or have all of its manufacturing plant achieve zero landfill).

- *Have you conducted an analysis of the environmental impact of your products and processes?* This requires the firm to conduct an LCA for its products and processes.

- *Do you have documented environmental objectives and targets?* Targets could be, for example, a 5 percent reduction in carbon footprint every two years, or a 5 percent reduction in yearly energy consumption in three years, etc. One of supermarket chain Tesco's environmental objectives is to reduce its CO_2 emissions per square foot of its stores and distribution centers by 50 percent by 2020, against a 2006 baseline.[12]

- *Have you established programs for achieving objectives and targets?* Programs are means to achieve targets. For example, the firm will retrofit all of its windows at its headquarters with energy-efficient ones; the firm will install solar panels in 30 percent of their retail locations in 5 years, etc.

- *Have you appointed personnel to oversee the implementation of the targets and programs?* Here, the firm needs to demonstrate accountability for the environmental targets and programs within the organization, including programs targeted toward compliance with environmental legislation.

- *Are the core elements of the EMS defined in either paper or electronic form?* This demonstrates the need for documentation of targets, programs, procedures, and responsibilities.
- *Are there procedures that ensure that the documents associated with the EMS are created and maintained consistently?*
- *Do you have procedures for defining responsibility for nonconformances and taking actions to mitigate them?*
- *Do you have procedures for informing personnel about the elements of the EMS?*
- *Do you have procedures for defining responsibility for nonconformances, and taking actions to mitigate them?*
- *Do you have procedures for periodic audits of the documents in the EMS?*

ISO 14001 was a standard created by the International Standards Organization (ISO) to evaluate the soundness of a firm's EMS. Thus, a firm can have its EMS certified against the ISO 14001 standard. Simply put, ISO 14001 is to an EMS what ISO 9000 is to quality management, so we first review some basic facts about ISO 9000.

Most firms have quality management programs; however, pursuing ISO 9000 Certification signals to the world that the firm's quality management system is sound, because it has been reviewed by an independent accreditation body against an international standard. ISO 9000 does not ensure that the firm's product has quality; it does ensure, however, that all processes within the firm (to design, produce, and distribute the product or service) are consistent. ISO 9000 Certification occurs at the site level, and not at the firm level—thus, a firm may have one plant that is ISO 9000 certified but not another plant. A study has shown that ISO 9000 Certification pays of financially: firms that pursue certification are better off—in terms of return on investment (ROI) and cost of goods sold (COGS) as a percentage of sales—than firms that do not pursue certification.[13] The improved financial performance is likely related to changes made in the firm's processes—in pursuing ISO 9000 Certifications, firms must take a hard look at their processes in order to document them; this exercise reveals "low-hanging fruit"—opportunities that can be targeted for improvement.

Just as a firm that is ISO 9000 certified does not necessarily produce high quality products, the products produced by a firm whose EMS is ISO 14001 certified are not necessarily "green." The ISO 14001 label only certifies that the firm has established a functioning EMS, according to international standards. In addition, ISO 14001 Certification does not state that the firm is in compliance with existing environmental regulations. It only states that that the firm has a well-defined process to comply with all relevant regulations. Corbett and Kirsch[14] have identified the following three myths about ISO 14001 Certification:

- *Myth 1: ISO 14000 is strictly an environmental standard, thus it is irrelevant to my business.* Some managers may have the wrong impression that ISO 14001 Certification is important primarily for firms with significant environmental risks, such as heavy manufacturing and processing industries. About one-third of all certified firms to date, however, are in service industries. There are potential benefits of ISO 14001 beyond improved environmental performance, as discussed in detail in myth 3 below.
- *Myth 2: ISO 14001 is a pain.* It is true that ISO 9000 certification may be indeed time consuming (typical implementation times are about 12–18 months) and expensive (considering all hours spent plus consulting fees, and Certification fees).

   ISO 14001 Certification is a natural extension of ISO 9000, since both standards use the plan-do-check-act planning cycle as discussed before. In addition, the scope of ISO 14001 is narrower (relative to ISO 9000), systems do not need to be perfect, and nonconformances are easier to remedy. The key message is: if a firm is already ISO 9000 certified, then it should also seek ISO 14001 Certification.

- *Myth 3: "There are no benefits to ISO 14001 Certification."* The benefits of ISO 14001 Certification can be described in three categories:

○ *Improved relationships with communities and authorities:* ISO 14001 Certification signals to communities and local governments that the firm has made a good faith effort to deal with environmental issues—for example, if accidents happen, then an ISO 14001 certified firm has a plan to deal with them. In addition, a carefully thought out EMS may decrease the probability of costly accidents, due to the planning and accountability procedures inherent in it. As a result, ISO 14001 certified firms may experience less intensive surveillance and monitoring by authorities, and faster granting of permits for expansion or construction projects.

○ *Organizational learning:* The process of formalizing procedures reduces the firm's dependence on a few key individuals. In addition, the requirement that employees be trained in the details of the firm's EMS may yield morale benefits.

○ *Financial benefits:* ISO 14001 Certification may result in cost reductions. Just as in the case with ISO 9000 Certification, being forced to take a detailed look at the firm's processes may reveal inefficiencies; the firm's costs associated with waste processing and removal are also likely to decrease. The firm may experience a higher market share, because its potential customers may only look for suppliers that are certified (similarly to some automotive firms that require ISO 9000 Certification as a condition for doing business with some suppliers). These financial benefits should be reflected in the firm's stock prices. In fact, a study found that financial markets react positively to the news of ISO 14001 Certification—median abnormal return (i.e., return above market return) for firms receiving certification was about 0.77 percent for the two days following certification.[15]

In fact, the same study has found that no company that has implemented ISO 14001 has regretted it.[16]

4.4   Green Buildings and LEED Certification

Among voluntary green labels and certifications a firm may pursue, an important one that has achieved a significant adoption rate is LEED certification for buildings. LEEDv4—Leadership in Energy and Environmental Design—is a rating system for buildings created by the U.S. Green Building Council (USGBC). Out of a maximum of 110 points for new construction and major renovations, the rating system awards points for buildings in seven major categories as follows (numbers mean the possible number of points to be awarded in each sub-category)[17]:

- Credit: Integrative Process 1

Location and Transportation (LT): 16 Possible Points

- LT Credit: LEED for Neighborhood Development Location 8-16
- LT Credit: Sensitive Land Protection 1
- LT Credit: High-Priority Site 1-2
- LT Credit: Surrounding Density and Diverse Uses 1-5
- LT Credit: Access to Quality Transit 1-5
- LT Credit: Bicycle Facilities 1
- LT Credit: Reduced Parking Footprint 1
- LT Credit: Green Vehicles 1

Sustainable Sites (SS): 10 Possible Points

- Prerequisite 1: Construction Activity Pollution Prevention (Required)
- SS Credit: Site Assessment 1
- SS Credit: Site Development—Protect or Restore Habitat 1-2
- SS Credit: Open Space 1
- SS Credit: Rainwater Management 2-3
- SS Credit: Heat Island Reduction 1-2
- SS Credit: Light Pollution Reduction 1

Water Efficiency (WE): 11 Possible Points

- Prerequisite 1: Outdoor Water Use Reduction (Required)
- Prerequisite 2: Indoor Water Use Reduction (Required)
- Prerequisite 3: Building-Level Water Metering (Required)
- WE Credit: Outdoor Water Use Reduction 1-2
- WE Credit: Indoor Water Use Reduction 1-6

- WE Credit Cooling Tower Water use 1-2
- WE Credit: Water Metering 1

Energy and Atmosphere (EA): 33 Possible Points

- Prerequisite 1: Fundamental Commissioning of Building (Required)
- Prerequisite 2: Minimum Energy Performance (Required)
- Prerequisite 3: Building-Level Energy Metering (Required)
- Prerequisite 4: Fundamental Refrigerant Management (Required)
- EA Credit: Enhanced Commissioning 2-6
- EA Credit: Optimize Energy Performance 1-18
- EA Credit: Advanced Energy Metering 1
- EA Credit: Demand Response 1-2
- EA Credit: Enhanced Refrigerant Management 1
- EA Credit: Renewable Energy Production 1-3
- EA Credit: Green Power and Carbon Offsets 1-2

Materials and Resources (MR): 13 Possible Points

- Prerequisite 1: Storage and Collection of Recyclables (Required)
- Prerequisite 2: Construction and Demolition Waste Management Planning (Required)
- MR Credit: Building Life-Cycle Impact Reduction 2-6
- MR Credit: Building Product Disclosure and Optimization—Environmental Product Declarations 1-2
- MR Credit: Building Product Disclosure and Optimization—Sourcing of Raw Materials 1-2
- MR Credit: Building Product Disclosure and Optimization—Material Ingredients 1-2
- MR Credit: Construction and Demolition Waste Management 1-2

Indoor Environmental Quality (EQ): 16 Possible Points

- Prerequisite 1: Minimum Indoor Air Quality Performance (Required)
- Prerequisite 2: Environmental Tobacco Smoke (ETS) Control (Required)
- EQ Credit: Enhanced Indoor Air Quality Strategies 1

- EQ Credit: Low-Emitting Materials 1-2
- EQ Credit: Construction Indoor Air Quality Management Plan 1
- EQ Credit: Indoor Air Quality Assessment 1
- EQ Credit: Thermal Comfort 1
- EQ Credit: Interior Lighting 1-2
- EQ Credit: Daylight 1-3
- EQ Credit: Quality Views 1
- EQ Credit: Acoustic Performance 1

Innovation (IN): 6 Possible Points

- IN Credit: Innovation 1-5
- IN Credit : LEED Accredited Professional 1

Regional Priority (RP): 4 Possible Points

- RP Credit: Regional Priority 1-4

For example, under Materials and Resources MR Credit: Construction and Demolition Waste Management, the requirement for being awarded the two possible points are as follows:

Recycle and/or salvage nonhazardous construction and demolition materials. Calculations can be by weight or volume but must be consistent throughout. Exclude excavated soil, land-clearing debris from calculations. Include materials destined for alternative daily cover (ADC) in the calculations as waste (not diversion). Include wood waste converted to fuel (biofuel) in the calculations; other types of waste-to-energy are not considered diversion for this credit . . . *Option 1: Diversion (1-2 points): Divert 50% and three material streams (1 Point); Divert 75% and four material streams (2 points). Option 2: Reduction of total Waste Material—Do not generate more than 2.5 pounds of construction waste per square foot.*

As another example, for water efficiency, the WE prerequisite indoor water use reduction stipulates that the design must use 20 percent less water than a baseline calculated for the building, where the standard provides specific guidelines for computing the baseline water consumption (e.g., 1.6 gallons per flush for commercial toilets, 1.0 gallons per flush for commercial urinals, 2.5 gallons per minute at 80 psi per shower stall for showerheads, etc.). The WE credit indoor water use reduction awards 1 point for each additional 5 percent indoor water reduction (from the 20 percent requirement), for a maximum of 6 points for 50 percent indoor water use reduction.

The standard also provides suggestions for possible technologies for achieving the points. For example, for Water Efficiency WE Credit: Indoor Water Use Reduction, some suggestions are:

> Further reduce fixture and fitting water use from the calculated baseline in WE Prerequisite Indoor Water Use Reduction. Additional potable water savings can be earned above the prerequisite level using alternative water sources. Include fixtures and fittings necessary to meet the needs of the occupants. Some of these fittings and fixtures may be outside the tenant space (for Commercial Interiors) or project boundary (for New Construction).

There are four levels of Certification, depending on the number of points achieved by the building:

- LEED certified: 40–49 points
- LEED Silver Certified: 50–59 points
- LEED Gold Certified: 60–79 points
- LEED Platinum certified: 80 points and above

As an example, the Bronx Library Center, in New York, is LEED Silver Certified. Among many other features, 90 percent of the demolition debris was recycled, the building achieves 20 percent energy cost savings (relative to a baseline for comparable buildings), and 80 percent of the wood used is Forest Stewardship Council (FSC) certified. (Green labels and Certifications are discussed further in Chapter 8.)

The popularity of LEED Certification is evident in Figure 4.6, which shows significant growth since its inception in 2000. In fact, LEED is

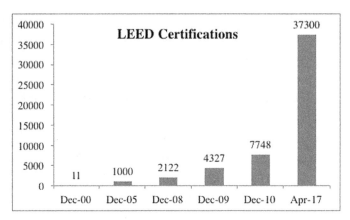

Figure 4.6 Growth in LEED certifications since its inception.

adopted outside of the United States, with projects in more than 160 countries, including Europe, Asia, and Latin America.[18]

Some of the features in green buildings, necessary for LEED certification, can be easily justified financially. For example, if a building consumes 20 percent less electricity than a baseline (comparable) building, the firm can estimate the net present value of these savings (by assuming a certain average cost of electricity, and the annual baseline consumption of electricity), and these savings can be compared with the upfront investments in technology necessary to achieve these savings (e.g., energy-efficient appliances and fixtures, photovoltaic solar panels). A significant portion of monetary savings used in justifying these projects, however, originates from improved employee productivity (working in a healthier environment, with better temperature, ventilation, indoor air quality, natural illumination), estimated to be around 5 percent for green buildings.[19]

4.5   Web Resources

Many of the topics discussed in this chapter are progressing rapidly, although some (such as LCA) are fairly mature. The reader can find additional resources (and constantly updated information) on the following sites:

- LCA: http://www.nrel.gov/lci/related_links.html
- Carbon footprinting standards: http://www.ghgprotocol.org
- Calculating one's carbon footprint: https://www3.epa.gov/carbon-footprint-calculator/
- ISO 14000: https://www.iso.org/iso-14001-environmental-management.html
- LEED Certification standards: http://www.usbc.org

CHAPTER 5

Closing the Loop—Design for the Environment (DfE)

5.1 General Guidelines for DfE

During the past 60 years or so, the industrial paradigm for the manufacturing of consumer goods has been to design and manufacture products for a single life cycle: minimizing material use (with the objective of minimizing variable production cost), so that products are less expensive but have to be discarded upon failure or obsolescence, rather than being repaired or reused. End-of-life, however, is only one stage of the life cycle of a product, as discussed in the last chapter. Broadly speaking, DfE means designing products that minimize environmental impact throughout their life cycle, including raw material extraction, transportation, manufacturing, packaging and distribution, use by consumers, and end-of-life. Moreover, environmental impact can also be defined in many different forms: materials choice (toxicity and/or scarcity), energy consumption, carbon footprint, solid waste, and so forth.

As a result of these multiple objectives, there are many different (and sometimes conflicting) guidelines for DfE. In this section, we outline a few broad principles of DfE, and comment on more specific DfE guidelines later in the chapter [such as packaging, design for remanufacturing, and cradle-to-cradle (C2C) design principles]. The broad principles of DfE can be described as follows:

- *Materials choice.* As discussed in Chapter 4 (in the subsection "Inventory Analysis and Impact Assessment"), a good design would use materials with ample supply on earth, low rates of depletion, high potential for recycling, and low or no toxicity. Under these criteria, recommended materials may include aluminum, iron, carbon, hydrogen, manganese, nitrogen, oxygen, silicon, and titanium. Using the same criteria, the designer should avoid silver, gold, arsenic, cadmium, chlorine, chromium, mercury, nickel, and lead.

- *Ease of disassembly.* A good design would have parts that can be easily disassembled. Disassembly should also be accomplished using commonly available tools. Ideally, parts after disassembly should be homogeneous in terms of materials, that is, they should be made of a single type of material. This facilitates recycling.

- *Minimize energy consumption.* Minimizing energy consumption during the life cycle requires different strategies for different products. As discussed earlier in the book, Internet routers consume the bulk of their electricity during the use stage of their life cycle. Consequently, energy-efficient designs are preferable for routers. In contrast, cell phones consume the bulk of their electricity during manufacturing. As a result, energy-efficient cell phones have limited beneficial impact on the environment; however, a cell phone that can be manufactured using recycled materials (secondary production usually consumes less energy than primary production), or that can reuse components that are energy intensive to manufacture will be more environmentally friendly.

- *Minimize solid residues.* A good design should generate fewer solid residues during its manufacturing. There are three types of solid residues[1]:
  - *Process residues:* They form as a result of the manufacturing process; examples include fly ash from coal combustion, and sludge. Processes should be designed so as to minimize these residues, and whenever possible, to find use for the sludge.
  - *Product residues:* These were intended to be part of the product. Examples include plastic molding, machining, powder metal (metal products that are made of compressed powder metal, and then heat treated; this process generates residues during pressing), and others. These residues are unavoidable; however, most residues should not be contaminated during the process so as to allow reuse and/or recycling.
  - *Packaging residues:* We discuss packaging later.

- *Minimize liquid residues:* A good design should generate few or no liquid residues during its manufacturing. Examples of liquid residues include trace-metal emissions to aquatic ecosystems (e.g., tanning of leather, industrial electroplating, smelting), and solvents and oils (e.g., stripping solutions used for cleaning metals for scale, and rust; waste water from dyeing processes, which contains salt, excess dyestuff, and other chemicals). As an example, Ciba launched its Cibacron LS (low salt), which is a type of dyestuff that reduces the consumption of salt necessary for dyeing by 75 percent; this also reduces the amount of water and wastewater residues.[2]

- *Standardization:* Standardization of components facilitates sorting and testing at the end of life, which are important steps in remanufacturing (as we discuss later).

- *Modular designs:* In a modular product design, the interfaces between components are not coupled (such that a design change in one component does not require design changes in other components), and usually each component only performs a single function. An example is Xerox copiers: at a higher level, there are three modules (paper input module, imaging module, and finishing module), with each module comprising sub-modules. Xerox copiers have a modular design, such that the same module can be reused in multiple generations of the product. Thus, a newer generation of the imaging module can be combined with the existing paper input and finishing modules to constitute a new product generation. A modular design is in direct contrast with an integral design, where interfaces are coupled, and some components perform multiple functions; integral designs (such as smartphones) optimize mass and volume. Modular designs are important for remanufacturing (as we discuss later), and they allow for easy upgrading of an older generation product to a newer generation one. Integral designs, however, may minimize material consumption, due to its optimization of mass and volume.

- Use of recycled materials: This point has been addressed in previous points, but it deserves further discussion. The process of recycling

materials typically consumes less energy than corresponding primary production, as seen in the previous chapter. The process of
recycling aluminum, for example, consumes 15 times less energy
than primary aluminum production through bauxite. The use of
recycled materials in designs is even more important for materials
that are not abundant on earth, such as nickel.

• *Recyclability of materials.* This was addressed before, in the general
category of materials choice, but again merits further discussion.
Some DfE protocols—such as cradle-to-cradle (C2C)—emphasize complete recyclability of materials as a key dimension of DfE.
C2C is based on the notion that "waste is food": products can
be easily disassembled and separated into homogeneous components; each component should be made of a single nontoxic
material. Further, each component can and should be completely
recycled for manufacturing of new components (i.e., there should
be "upcycling" as opposed to "downcycling"). We discuss C2C
later in this chapter.

5.2   Packaging Design and Packaging Scorecards

According to the U.S. EPA,[3] each person generates 4.4 lbs of municipal
solid waste (MSW) *per day* in the United States, of which 1.52 lbs
are recycled, 0.56 lbs are recovered in the form of energy, and 2.32 lbs are
sent to landfills. In terms of materials, paper and paperboard comprise
27 percent of all materials (by weight, before recycling) in MSW, followed by food scraps (15 percent), yard trimmings (13 percent), plastics
(13 percent), rubber, lead and textiles (10 percent), metals (9 percent),
wood (6 percent), and glass (4 percent). MSW overall recycling rates have
increased from 16 percent in 1990 to 35 percent in 2014; recycling rates
for corrugated boxes, glass, metals, and plastic are currently 90 percent,
26 percent, 34 percent, and 10 percent, respectively. In terms of products,
a significant portion of waste is comprised of containers and packaging, at
30 percent, as seen in Figure 5.1. Therefore, sustainable packaging is another
critical component of DfE.

Walmart has been an important force in driving sustainable packaging practices in its supply chain. In its Sustainable Packaging Playbook,

Walmart outlines the following packaging priorities, which contribute toward a supplier's sustainability index[4]:

- *Protect the product.* Design packaging that meets product protection International Safe Transit Authority (ISTA) standards while using the minimum amount of packaging.
- *Reduce materials.* Source reduce by eliminating packaging components or layers, "right sizing" packaging, and shifting to reusable containers.
- *Maximize recycled and sustainably sourced renewable content.* Increase the use of recycled and sustainably sourced renewable content.
- *Enhance material health.* Identify if you have priority chemicals in packaging.
- *Design for recycling.* Work with the Sustainable Packaging Coalition and the Association of Plastic Recyclers to design for recycling.
- *Communicate recyclability.* Use consumer-friendly recycling labels that meet U.S. Federal Trade Commission (FTC) Green Guides, such as the How2Recycle label.

Walmart, along with partner ECRM®, had developed a packaging scorecard. The scorecard is based on four key concepts: (i) what packaging

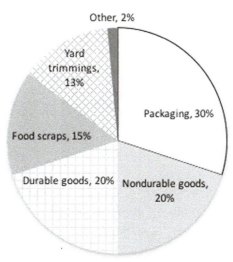

Figure 5.1 *Composition of municipal solid waste (MSW) in the United States in 2014. (Source: U.S. EPA)*

Table 5.1 Example of packaging scorecard for transport packaging

1. Packaging standards			
	1.1 Does the packaging conform to any packaging standards (e.g., MIL-STD)? (Y/N)		
	1.2 If so, what standards? Please list below		
2. Use of previously recycled materials			
	2.1 Estimate the percentage of packaging materials that consists of previously recycled content		
3. Product to package fit			
	3.1 Estimate what proportion of the package is occupied by the filler material that is not the actual product		
4. Materials Selection			
	4.1 Estimate the percentage (by volume) of the following materials used in the packaging		
		Percentage	Material Type
		_____	Any type of non-biodegradable packaging foam (e.g., Styrofoam)
			Corrugated cardboard
			Wood
		_____	Air-cellular cushioning (e.g., dunnage bags, Fill-Air® bags, bubble wrap)
		_____	Anti-static/electro-sensitive device (ESD) bags
			Shrink packaging (e.g., shrink wrap)
		_____	Paper packaging (e.g., PadPak® paper, FillPak® paper)
		100%	Total Percentage
5. Packaging return			
	5.1 Is there any procedure to return packaging for reuse/recycling? (Y/N)		
	5.2 Estimate the proportion of packages returned for reuse/recycling.		

(*Source:* University of Maryland QUEST)

material is used, (ii) how much of each material is used, (iii) how far the packaging component traveled before being filled, and (iv) how efficiently available space is utilized. The scorecard has been folded into the supplier's sustainability index.

Packaging includes both for the *selling unit* (packaging taken home by consumer from the retail location) and for *transport packaging* (packaging used to ship selling units to a retail location, which is discarded at the retail location).

An example of what a packaging scorecard for transport packaging may look like is shown in Table 5.1. Transport packaging is more important (than selling unit packaging) for a non-retailer, for example, an Original Equipment Manufacturer (e.g., Lockheed Martin, General Motors) analyzing transport packaging from its suppliers. Using a weighing system, the firm can create a single score for each supplier/package, by weighing the answers given in questions 2.1, 3.1, 4.1, and 5.2. The weights given to each of the different components of 4.1 (materials choice) would depend on how easy each of these materials is to recycle, or what percentage the firm is actually able to recycle in the current scenario.

5.3   Design for Remanufacturing

We now turn our attention to design principles for remanufacturing. We again stress that not all product types should be designed for remanufacturing. Remanufacturing, from a purely environmental perspective, is appropriate for products whose largest life cycle environmental impacts occur during raw material extraction and manufacturing, because that is where remanufacturing provides most of the savings (in terms of energy and materials). Thus, *it is not always advantageous for an OEM to design products that are easy to remanufacture*, from both environmental and economic perspectives:

- *Environmental aspect:* Products whose largest environmental impact is during use by consumers benefit from having the most up-to-date energy-efficient technology, with environmentally friendly materials that can be completely recycled; in these cases, remanufacturing older technologies (and materials) may not be appropriate.
- *Economic aspect:* there are at least three reasons why an OEM would not want to design products that are easy to remanufacture.
  - *Technological obsolescence:* Technology improves very fast in some industries, precluding remanufacturing of end-of-use products that are too "obsolete," except for niche markets and

applications. Examples include old computers and cell phones. Consumer returns, on the other hand, allow remanufacturing even for these fast-moving industries due to their relative low usage; remanufacturing in those cases, however, is a relatively simple operation, consisting mostly of cosmetic repairs and software updates.

○ *Fashion products:* Engines and transmissions (not subject to fashion) are remanufactured, but not parts from an automobile's interior or exterior, which are normally recycled (unless they can be remanufactured for use in spare parts).

○ *Who reaps the rewards of remanufacturing?* In products such as printer cartridges, third-party firms are the ones that reap the rewards of an OEM designing products that are easy to remanufacture. OEMs understand this, and under these circumstances design products for recycling, as opposed to remanufacturing; OEMs actually design products that make it hard to remanufacture (for example, some chips that electronically disable refilled printer cartridges).

In this section, we focus on broad design principles for remanufacturing where it makes sense. As we discuss in more detail in Chapter 7, remanufacturing typically involves the following steps:

• *Product acquisition:* Obtaining used products (also known as cores).
• *Testing and sorting:* Assessing condition of used products, sorting, and categorizing them (e.g., bad, good, better, best).
• *Remanufacturing process:* Disassembly, cleaning, parts repair or renewal, reassembly, and testing.
• Remarketing of the remanufactured product.

Design for remanufacturing addresses some or all of these steps. The principles outlined in this section are based on a compilation by Bert Bras.[5] In a nutshell, the goal is to design a product that:

1. Will be returned to the producer in an easy and inexpensive way,
2. Can be easily sorted,

3. Has a large number of reusable components,

4. Requires minimal disassembly effort, and

5. Allows for easy and inexpensive remanufacturing.

The guidelines can be categorized in terms of product architecture, maintenance and repair guidelines, sorting and testing guidelines, disassembly and reassembly guidelines, cleaning, repair and reconditioning guidelines.

Product Architecture Guidelines

Modular product architecture—where there is a 1:1 correspondence between component and function, and whose interfaces between components are not coupled—is preferred, because it allows for easy replacement of obsolete or damaged modules or components with new ones. Components that are good candidates for remanufacturing include those with stable technology, that are damage resistant, and for which aesthetics and fashion are largely irrelevant. Classical designs are preferred, to alleviate issues with fashion. Finally, "sturdy," damage-resistant designs are recommended: Bras[6] provides an example of a particular clutch pressure plate, which is a heavy component that can be easily remanufactured; however, its non-sturdily designed plate ears—used for attaching the plate to adjacent components—could be easily broken during removal and handling. This weak link in the plate design compromised remanufacturing because a plate with a broken ear could be repaired only using an expensive welding process, rendering it uneconomical.

Maintenance and Repair Guidelines

For remanufacturing to be economically attractive, cores—used products acquired—should be in good condition. Thus, good maintenance and repair during the product's use are critical. Products should have clear guidelines to users on how the product should be opened for cleaning and repair (e.g., Xerox copiers). If possible, information on parts requiring periodic maintenance should be displayed on the product itself (as opposed to in a user's manual); an example is tire pressure stickers on automobile doors. Finally, if possible, the designer should locate parts that wear out quickly close to one another, as this facilitates service.

Sorting and Testing Guidelines

After product acquisition, the remanufacturer must sort products (into different product types and condition) and test them. Standardization (of components, fasteners, interfaces, and tools) and reduced product proliferation is recommended here. Bras[7] provides an example of a large automotive remanufacturer in the Atlanta area that dealt with 3,400 different part numbers for brake products in 1983; that number increased to 16,500 in 1995 due to product proliferation. In light of this proliferation, designers should provide clear visual distinctions that allow for easy recognition of different part numbers, to facilitate sorting.

Disassembly and Reassembly Guidelines

Disassembly and reassembly times should be short, so as to minimize disassembly cost and make remanufacturing economical. Preferably, the product should have a "base" for locating and inserting other components; ideally the base should not need to be re-positioned or rotated during disassembly and reassembly. Components should be symmetrical to the extent possible, avoiding unique left/ right components. When fasteners are needed, the designer should:

- Avoid permanent fasteners that require destructive removal (e.g., rivets or welds). When permanent fasteners cannot be avoided, they should be applied in a way that their removal does not damage the core of the product.
- Increase corrosion resistance of fasteners.
- Standardize fasteners to the extent possible so that one or fewer tools are needed during assembly and disassembly.

Cleaning, Repair, and Reconditioning Guidelines

The designer should use materials that do not degrade during the cleaning process (typical cleaning processes include chemical bath and sand blasting) in remanufacturing. The designer should also look for ways to minimize the number of parts subject to wear and tear (which require replacement, increasing remanufacturing cost). Some products do not require full disassembly (to the component level) for cleaning and repair in remanufacturing; in that case the disassembly sequence should be such that parts needing repair and replacement can be reached quickly. For parts that need recoating and/or repainting, the designer should minimize the number of orifices that must be masked during coating and/or painting, as well as minimize the number of parts that must be removed prior to recoating and repainting.

In sum, the idea in designing for remanufacturing is to design a product that is easy to disassemble, sort, clean, repair, and reassemble, and that has a large proportion (in dollar terms) of reusable components.

5.4   Cradle-to-Cradle® Design Principles

The principles of Cradle-to-Cradle® (C2C) design originate from William McDonough, an American architect, and Michael Braungart, a German chemist. They are inspired by the existing cycles of nature, where "waste is food": waste from a living organism becomes food for other living organisms. Most other DfE principles are based on the notion of eco-efficiency, where the designer improves existing designs and processes so as to reduce a product's environmental impact through its life cycle: designs minimize the use of toxic materials, energy consumption, the amount of scarce materials, the amount of waste during manufacturing and end-of-life, and so forth. C2C is based on the principle of eco-effectiveness, where products should be designed in a way that they eliminate environmental impact: no use of toxic materials, and the products can be *easily disassembled* into *homogeneous components* made of a single type of material that can be *upcycled* (i.e., recycled to be used in the manufacturing of the same components). Notice the contrast between upcycling (as required by C2C) and downcycling, where materials lose some of their properties during the recycling process and can only be used in alternative applications (e.g., recycled plastic used in park benches; recycled paper used in newspapers or toilet paper).

In eco-efficient systems, less is better: the lower the amount of products made with toxic materials, the lower the amount of waste released during the product's manufacturing and end of life, the better it is for the environment. This is in contrast with eco-Effective systems—according to McDonough and Braungart[8]:

> If nature adhered to the human model of efficiency, there would be fewer cherry blossoms, and fewer nutrients. Fewer trees, less oxygen, and less clean water. Fewer songbirds. Less diversity, less creativity, and delight. The idea of nature being more efficient, dematerializing, or even not "littering" (imagine zero waste or zero emissions for nature!) is preposterous. The marvelous thing about effective systems is that one wants more of them, not less. (p. 77)

> The key is not to make human industries and systems smaller, as efficiency advocates propound, but to design them to get bigger and better in a way that replenishes, restores, and nourishes the rest of the world. Thus, the right things for manufacturers and industrialists to do are those that lead to good growth—more niches, health, nourishment, diversity, intelligence and abundance—for this generation of inhabitants on the planet and for generations to come. (p. 78)

A product design can be certified to be C2C compliant, and to that end it should meet certain criteria. There are five levels of certification: basic, bronze, silver, gold, and platinum. The complete set of criteria is available at www.c2ccertified.org, and can be summarized for version 3.1 (2017) as[9]:

- *Biological and technical nutrients.* There are two fundamentally different types of materials that can be used in product design. Biological nutrients are biodegradable, and can be safely composted after use; examples include cotton and leather tanned with vegetable tanning. Technical nutrients are the materials used in the industrial cycle: they are not biodegradable but can be upcycled and reused in the manufacturing of the same new products. Examples include steel, aluminum, precious metals, some plastics, etc. C2C emphasizes that the two types of materials should be kept separate, and "monstrous hybrids" should not be created. A "**monstrous hybrid**" would be a product component made of both technical and biological nutrients, where both materials cannot be easily separated and salvaged after their current lives. An example would include a conventional leather shoe that is tanned with chromium. The leather itself is a biological nutrient, but the chromium is a technical nutrient: it is a scarce and valuable material that cannot be upcycled when it is part of the leather shoe. In C2C Certification, at all levels, all materials must be identified as *either* biological or technical nutrients.

• *Material health.* Materials are classified into six levels, according to their risk and toxicity to humans and the environment. *Green materials* (A and B levels) pose little or no risk (such as aluminum or steel), and are preferred. *Yellow materials* (C) pose low to moderate risk (such as halogenated hydrocarbon), and are acceptable for continued use unless a green material alternative exists. *Red materials* (X) pose high risk (such as PVC), and should be phased out. *Gray materials* have incomplete data, and their level of risk cannot be assessed. Black materials are banned from use in certified products (e.g., mercury, flame retardants) At all C2C Certification levels, all material ingredients need to be identified at the 100 ppm level (0.01 percent), and assessed according to their health in terms of green, yellow, and red (A, B, C, and X); in addition, there should be no PVC, or chloroprene at any concentration. A product certified at the silver level should have 95 percent of its materials (by weight) assessed using ABC-X ratings. At the gold certification level, there can be no red assessed materials. At the platinum level, all process chemicals have been assessed, with none assessed as X.

• *Material reutilization.* This is assessed according to the material reutilization score (MRS): MRS = [(% Recyclable/ Compostable Content)*2 + (% Recycled/Renewed Content)*1]/3. At the bronze certification level, the MRS should be greater than 35. At the silver certification level, the MRS score should be greater than 50; at the gold level, the MRS score should be greater than 65, and at the platinum level, the MRS score should be 100. In addition, at the gold and platinum levels, the firm must have a well-defined plan for developing logistics and recovery systems for the product. At the platinum level, the product can be recovered, and remanufactured into a new product of equal or higher value.

- *Renewable energy use.* Manufacturers must commit to the use of solar, wind, geothermal, or other renewable sources of energy. At the bronze certification level, manufacturers must quantify and characterize the energy used in the product's final assembly. At the silver and gold level, greater than 5 percent, and 50 percent, respectively, of the energy used in the product's final assembly should be from renewable sources. At the platinum level, 100 percent of the energy used in the product's final assembly should be from renewable sources, and 5 percent of the product's entire energy footprint is covered by offsets.

- *Water stewardship.* The water leaving the factory should be as clean as or cleaner than when it came in. At the silver certification level, product-related process chemicals are characterized and assessed. At the gold level, product-related process chemicals are optimized. At the platinum level, all water leaving the facility meets drinking water standards.

- *Social responsibility.* Respecting the diversity of people and cultures is a key principle of C2C. C2C is based on adaptation of the firm's business practices to locally available resources, and local people and their cultures. At the bronze certification level, a full social responsibility self-audit is complete and a positive impact strategy is developed. At the silver level, supply chain-relevant social issues are fully investigated and a positive strategy is developed. At the gold level, the firm must conduct self-assessment toward a third-party certification of social responsibility. At the platinum level, the firm must complete a third-party certification of social responsibility.

As seen above, the criteria for C2C Certification are very stringent, and to date, relatively few complex products have been certified. For example, for office furniture, there were examples by Ahrend, Allsteel, and Steelcase.[10] There are many more examples of "simpler" products (i.e., not comprised and assembled of too many different parts), such as construction products (e.g., siding, flooring, insulation), body cleansers, textiles, and housewares, that are also certified.

5.5   Web Resources

The following links provide more in-depth information about some of the topics covered in this chapter, in addition to frequent updates:

- U.S. EPA's Safer Choice Program: https://www.epa.gov/saferchoice
- DfE guidelines for different industries: http://www.iisd.org/business/tools/bt_dfe.aspx
- Cradle-to-cradle and Certification: http://www.mbdc.com
- OECD's toolbox for material substitution: http://www.oecdsaatoolbox.org

CHAPTER 6

Servicizing and Leasing

6.1   Introduction: Servicizing vs. Leasing

In the previous chapter, we discussed the difference between biological and technical nutrients. The Cradle-to-Cradle® design protocol indicates that biological nutrients (biodegradable items) can be safely returned to the earth and composted, whereas technical nutrients (such as steel, aluminum, plastic) should be upcycled—designed to be recycled in a way that the material does not lose any of its technical properties, and can be used to produce the same product (or better) again. Thus, products are designed such that technical nutrients can be reused for (theoretically) an infinite number of times. McDonough and Braungart indicate one way for this scenario to be practically feasible: firms should have control of the product after the end of their use by consumers—that is, firms should sell the service the product provides, not the ownership of the product. In their words[1]:

> In order for such a scenario to be practical, however, we have to introduce a concept that goes hand in hand with the notion of a technical nutrient: the concept of a *product of service*. Instead of assuming that all products are to be bought, owned, and disposed of by "consumers," products containing valuable technical nutrients—cars, televisions, carpeting, computers, and refrigerators, for example—would be reconceived as services people want to enjoy. In this scenario, customers (a more apt term for users of these products) would effectively purchase the service of such a product for a *defined user period*—say, 10,000 hours of television viewing, rather than the television itself.

Thus, McDonough and Braungart posit that *servicizing* is inherently green—as long as the product is designed in such a way that technical and biological nutrients can be easily separated, and there are no "monstrous hybrids."

There are many different business models for manufacturing firms that sell a service instead of selling a product, but we can consider two types here, leasing and servicizing, which are fundamentally different, especially in the way that the customer is charged for the service. A *leasing* agreement is like a rental, where the firm rents the product to the customer for a relatively long period of time, such as years, and the customer *pays a fixed fee per period*, typically monthly, *independent of the usage*. The product stays with the customer, and is returned at the end of the lease. Some examples of leasing are presented later. In contrast, in a *servicizing* model, *the customer pays the firm only for the exact amount of the product used*. For example, Xerox offers a service where the customer pays only for the number of pages printed. Similarly, many cloud computing and storage services are charged by usage. Finally, car sharing services such as ZipCar are ubiquitous in larger cities, as well as bike sharing services.

6.2   Are Servicizing and Leasing Always Green?

First, consider servicizing. The following arguments support the environmental superiority of servicizing over the usual model of selling products[2]:

1. Since customers are charged by the amount they use the product, they may be incentivized to use less, which reduces energy consumption during the use stage of the life cycle.
2. Under some servicizing models, the firm does not provide each customer with a dedicated product; customers draw from a pool of products. Such pooling means that the customers' needs are met with fewer units, which means there is lower production, hence reducing environmental impact during the production stage of the life cycle. For example, not all ZipCar users need to own a car, which reduces the amount of cars produced by the manufacturers.
3. The manufacturer may be incentivized to design and manufacture products with higher efficiency, as it lowers its operating costs.

Again, this lowers the environmental impact during the use stage of the life cycle.

There are arguments, however, that also suggest that servicizing may not be greener[3]:

1. Because the manufacturer charges customers by usage, it may reach customers who would not otherwise be able to afford (and use) the product, thus increasing total usage, and hence a higher total environmental impact during the use stage of the life cycle.
2. Although pooling may decrease the production volume, it also allows the manufacturer to charge a lower price, and hence increase adoption and use, thus increasing the total environmental impact during the use stage of the life cycle.
3. A more efficient product reduces the firm's operating costs, and hence allows it to charge a lower price, increasing adoption and usage. This increases the total environmental impact during the use stage of the life cycle.

Now, consider leasing. The main argument for leasing as a green business model is that it promotes reuse: end-of-lease equipment is still functional, and can be reused as-is (as is the case with cars, for example), or can be refurbished for a new life. Xerox is an example of a firm that designs products for multiple generations. Products have a modular design, and "sturdy" frames that can be reused with little rework, after the end of the leasing period with customers. Thus, a Xerox copier returned from the customer after leasing expiration can be easily upgraded (through the modular design, which allows easy replacement of obsolete modules with new ones) to a newer product generation, after the remanufacturing process.

Realistically speaking, however, few products are designed in a way that makes it feasible (technically and/or economically) to completely upcycle the materials for reuse in the manufacturing of equivalent new products. Thus, there exist some arguments indicating that leasing might not be greener than selling under some scenarios. These are shown in Table 6.1.

The first point in Table 6.1 is particularly important, because in practice, few firms design products in a way that makes recovery after lease economically and environmentally attractive. Firms vary significantly in their level of recovery activities, as well as the design of their products. Some examples are shown in Figure 6.1, and discussed below.

Table 6.1 Reasons why leasing might not be greener than selling

Reason	Explanation
Premature disposal of the product by manufacturer	• Remanufacturing end-of-lease products is an alternative to recycling for materials reuse. Some leasing firms may opt for prematurely ending a product life cycle (i.e., prematurely disposing the end-of-lease product, which could have another life after remanufacturing) for fear that the remanufactured product cannibalizes sales of corresponding new products. The midlife disposal of the product may result in more products being produced, and more being disposed overall than under a selling situation, which may make leasing environmentally worse.[4]
Consumers value resale value of a product if there is an active secondary market	• When customers buy a durable product (such as a car), they take into account its resale value, if there is a secondary market for the product. Thus, customers are willing to pay a higher price for a product that is more durable (which has a higher resale value). This may provide an incentive for manufacturers to design more durable products, with a higher resale value if they sell the product (as opposed to designing a less durable product when they lease it).[5]
Leasing may create a lack of ownership among users	• When customers buy durable products for which there is a secondary market, they invest in care and maintenance of the products, because that yields higher resale values. With leasing, the opposite may occur—the lack of ownership has the inverse effect.
Operating leases restricted to a length of 75 percent of the product's useful life	• In operating leases (where the lessor retains ownership of the product; see next section), the length of the lease is restricted to a maximum of 75 percent of the product's useful life. Thus, under operating leases, the lessor ("landlord") may dispose of a product with more than 25 percent of its useful life remaining (if it is not economically feasible to recycle it or remanufacture it), implying a higher rate of production and disposal overall. This point is related to the "premature disposal of the product by the manufacturer" above.

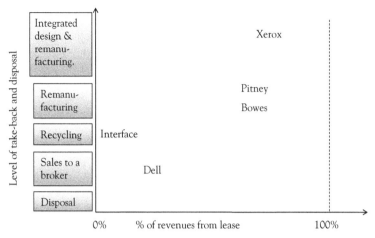

Figure 6.1 Firms vary in their level of recovery activities.

- **Dell**, the computer manufacturer, derives a small percentage of its revenue from leasing, and it does not engage significantly in remanufacturing of its end-of-lease units. Technological obsolescence presents a challenge in remanufacturing older equipment, and current processes for e-waste recycling make it difficult to upcycle materials (particularly not only plastics, but also some metals).

- **Interface** is a carpet manufacturer, specialized in a modular carpet design, where the carpet is manufactured and installed in tiles. Thus, the customer has the ability to "mix and match" different designs, and also has the ability to selectively replace carpet tiles that are worn out (as opposed to the entire carpet, as in the traditional broadloom carpet). Interface also had a limited carpet leasing program, but where financing was done primarily through a third party. The leasing program at Interface was limited not so much due to a deliberate strategic choice by Interface, but due to most customers' reluctance in leasing carpet, where the leasing payments become an operational expense (as opposed to a one-time capital expenditure), and the carpet was reclaimed at the end of the leasing period (when the carpet still has more than 25 percent of its useful life remaining), which may inconvenience customers. Interface has developed, however, a breakthrough process for recycling carpet—the process, named ReEntry, allows for a clean mechanical separation between the backing (typically made of vinyl or polypropylene) and facing (made of Nylon 6 or Nylon 6,6), allowing both materials to be upcycled and used in the production of new carpet,[6] forming a true closed-loop system.

- **Pitney Bowes (PB)** is an OEM that manufactures mailing equipment used in businesses, for large-scale mailing (such as those used in a marketing campaign). PB offers leasing for most (80–90 percent) of its production of new equipment, with a typical leasing period of four years. At the end of a lease, PB's customers may upgrade to newer equipment if available. Used equipment is returned to PB, which may be remanufactured and re-sold or re-leased as a cheaper alternative to new products. We also discuss PB in Chapter 7.

- **Xerox** designs products with the intent of reusing it through multiple life cycles, through a modular design and "sturdy" designs, as discussed before.

Of course, there are other aspects of leasing (other than environmental) that may make it attractive to businesses, and we discuss some of the more conventional arguments for leasing (as opposed to selling) in the next section. The World Leasing Handbook estimated that leasing worldwide accounted for more than $1 trillion in 2015 (up from $650 million in 2010); North America makes up 41 percent of the leasing volume worldwide, with Europe, and Asia accounting for 32 percent, 22 percent of the world volume, respectively.

6.3   Types of Lease: Operating and Capital Lease

From an accounting perspective, there are two basic types of leases:

- *Operating lease.* The *lessor* ("landlord") enjoys the rewards and bears the risk of asset ownership. Payments are fixed, and as a result the lessor bears the risks (or rewards) associated with interest rates. The lessor is also responsible for recovering the value at the end of the lease, and there is thus technological risk. Operating leases are treated as "operating expenses," and as a result they are not treated as an asset in the lessee's balance sheet, which improves the lessee's Return on Assets (ROA).

• *Capital lease.* Here, the *lessee* enjoys the rewards and bears the risk of asset ownership. Thus, a capital lease is the simultaneous acquisition of a long-term asset, and a long-term liability corresponding to the lease payments.

The Financial Accounting Standards Board (FASB) has specific requirements for leases to be treated as capital or operational, and they are listed in Table 6.2. If the lease meets none of the four conditions listed in Table 6.2, then the lease should be treated as an operating lease. The distinction between operating and capital leases is important, because of financial accounting and reporting implications, as we discuss next.

In general, in addition to the (potential) environmental benefits, the economic arguments for firms to start offering a leasing model include:

• *Potential tax savings to both lessor and lessee.* Operating lease payments are considered as operating expenses to the lessor, and fully taxable revenues to the lessee. Because ownership is retained by the lessor in operating leases, the lessor writes of depreciation. Thus, if the lessor is in a higher tax bracket than the lessee, both benefit, as the lessor enjoys a higher depreciation write-off than the lessee would if it had ownership of the product (i.e., if the product was sold as opposed to leased). In addition, financial accounting reporting is simplified for the lessee in operating leases, as there is

Table 6.2 A Lease meeting any (or more) of these four conditions implies a capital lease

Nr	Condition (Meeting any one or more of these conditions implies a capital lease)
1	Asset ownership is transferred to the lessee at the end of the lease term
2	Transfer of ownership is likely due to a "bargain purchase" clause at the end of the lease (i.e., less than fair market value)
3	The lease extends for at least 75 percent of the asset's life
4	The present value of the minimum contractual lease payments equals or exceeds 90 percent of the fair market value of the product at the time lessee signs the contract

no need to include leased equipment depreciation in its financial reporting.

- *Leases enable lessees to spread out payments.* It becomes easier for lessees to make large capital investments, and that may increase demand for the lessor's products.

- *Additional revenue opportunities for lessor.* Leasing contracts frequently provide the lessor with the ability to add other services, such as maintenance, increasing revenues.

- *Leasing provides a stable source of revenue for lessor.* Because leasing is a long-term agreement, as opposed to a one-time transaction, it is more resilient to economic downturns.

- *Leasing allows for closer customer relationships.* Closer relationships with customers have the potential to increase follow-on business opportunities and contracts for the lessor.

- *Leasing allows for greater control of product resale.* As discussed above, the lessor retains ownership and control of the product at the time the lease expires, which provides the lessor with more control of the secondary market. For example, the lessor may decide to remanufacture end-of-lease products, which gives the lessor greater control over the quality of the remanufacturing process. This results in greater and more consistent quality of the lessor's remanufactured products, which helps to protect its brand. In contrast, when the customer buys the product, he/she has control of the product's resale; as a result, the product may end up in the hands of low quality third-party remanufacturers, which may be damaging to the OEM's brand.

In the next section, we provide an example of a simple financial analysis to illustrate the benefits and pitfalls of a leasing model (as opposed to a selling model) to both lessors and lessees.

6.4   A Spreadsheet Analysis of Leasing versus Buying Decision

In this section, we provide a simple example that illustrates some of the accounting issues highlighted in the previous section, particularly how operating leases are included in the lessor's balance sheet (but not in the lessee, being then treated as an operating expense). The example is hypothetical but representative of a scenario where Indiana University (IU) considers the acquisition of a large-scale mailing machine from PB, which will be used by the University for its mailing campaigns (e.g., promotions, fund raising, mailing admissions materials or letters, etc.). The useful life of the machine is eight years, but IU would move to a newer technology after five years. IU is considering whether to buy or to lease the machine:

- Buy: IU can simply buy the machine from PB for $52,000. IU needs to spend $600 per year in labor for regular maintenance, and $2,000 in replacement parts starting in the third year after acquisition of the machine (these parts will be acquired from PB). At the end of five years, IU can sell the used machine to a broker for $5,000.

- Lease: IU can lease the machine from PB for a period of five years. This is an operating lease. Monthly leasing payments are $1,000. In addition, IU must buy a maintenance program offered by PB for $2,200 per year, which covers both labor and parts. At the end of the leasing period, the machine is then sent back to PB, which can remanufacture it; the used machine has a salvage value to PB of $7,000.

Assume that PB's cost of goods sold (COGS) is 55 percent, and that its corporate income tax is 35 percent (IU, being a non-profit organization, has a 0 percent corporate tax rate). The data are summarized in Table 6.3.

The depreciation schedule used is the Modified Accelerated Cost Recovery System (MACRS) with a 2.0 declining balance method, which is generally used for income tax reporting purposes, and thus appropriate for estimating tax savings from depreciation. The MACRS depreciation schedule is 20 percent, 32 percent, 19.2 percent, 11.5 percent, 11.5 percent, and 5.8 percent for years 1, 2, 3, 4, 5, and 6, respectively (the MACRS system assumes firms acquire depreciable assets at the midpoint of the first year, regardless of the acquisition date; there is thus depreciation carrying to half of year 6).

Table 6.3 Data for leasing versus selling analysis for PB/IU example

Parameter description	Value
Lease term	5 years
Monthly lease payment	$1,000
Yearly discount rate	10%
Income tax rate (PB)	35%
Annual maintenance cost (PB: contractual offer)	$2,200.00
Annual maintenance cost (IU: labor only)	$600.00
Annual maintenance cost (IU: replacement parts purchased from PB; after year 2)	$2,000.00
Equipment price	$52,000.00
Salvage value after 5 years: IU	$5,000.00
Salvage value after 5 years: PB	$7,000.00
PB cost of goods sold (COGS)	55%

We select our time unit to be years. To keep it simple, we use a yearly discount rate of 10 percent for the purposes of computing net present value (NPV). The results are shown in Table 6.4 for IU, and in Table 6.6 for PB. We use the standard Excel convention that cash flows are presented at the end of the period, for simplicity, and traditional accounting convention that negative cash flows (i.e., expenses) are shown in parenthesis.

Indiana University Analysis

The formulas in Table 6.4 are straightforward, but we point out a few things. IU buys the machine at the beginning of year 1, or, alternatively, at the end of year 0. The NPV formula in cell B28 is given by =NPV(0.10,C27:G27)+B27, where 0.10 is the discount rate (10 percent) for NPV calculations in this example. Annual lease expense is $12,000, as the monthly lease payments are $1,000. The formula in cell B36 is simply the NPV of the lease-only payments (i.e., not including maintenance), that is =NPV(0.10,C32:G32). The formula in cell B37 represents the ratio between the NPV of the lease payments, and the cost of the machine (buy) at year 0, that is, 45,489/52,000, which yields 0.87; this ratio is below 90 percent, which is necessary for an operational lease. We see that

Table 6.4 Indiana university lease versus buy analysis

		A	B	C	D	E	F	G
22	Buying option	Year 0	Year 1	Year 2	Year 3	Year 4	Year 5
23	Initial cost	($52,000)	$ –	$ –	$ –	$ –	$ –
24	Maintenance: parts	$ –	$ –	$ –	($2,000)	($2,000)	($2,000)
25	Maintenance: labor	$ –	($600)	($600)	($600)	($600)	($600)
26	Salvage	$ –	$ –	$ –	$ –	$ –	$5,000
27	Total	($52,000)	($600)	($600)	($2,600)	($2,600)	$2,400
28	NPV	($55,280)					
29							
30							
31	Leasing option		Year 1	Year 2	Year 3	Year 4	Year 5
32	Annual lease expense		($12,000)	($12,000)	($12,000)	($12,000)	($12,000)
33	PB maintenance expense		($2,200)	($2,200)	($2,200)	($2,200)	($2,200)
34	Total		($14,200)	($14,200)	($14,200)	($14,200)	($14,200)
35	NPV	($53,829)					
36	NPV-lease only	($45,489)					
37	Lease/buy ratio	0.87					
38							
39	Preference for lease	$1,451					

the NPV of the buying option is ($55,280), whereas the NPV of the leasing option is $53,829, which implies that the leasing option is cheaper by $1,451 over the five-year planning horizon. Notice that there are no depreciation calculations for IU under the buying option, as the firm pays zero corporate income tax.

Pitney Bowes (PB) Analysis

The first step here is to calculate the tax savings from depreciation. Because this is an operating lease, the machine "stays" in PB's balance sheet as a depreciable asset. This is shown in Table 6.5.

The capital value (base) for depreciation is the cost of goods sold at PB, which is equal to 52,000 × 0.55, or $28,600 (cell B73). The

Table 6.5 Depreciation calculations for PB

71	A	B	C	D	E	F	G	H
72	Depreciation calculation for PB (Leasing)							
73	Capital value (COGS)	$28,600	Year 1	Year 2	Year 3	Year 4	Year 5	Year 6
74	Depreciation schedule		20.0%	32.0%	19.2%	11.5%	11.5%	5.8%
75	Depreciation		$5,720	$9,152	$5,491	$3,289	$3,289	$1,659
76	Depreciation tax savings		$2,002	$3,203	$1,922	$1,151	$1,151	$581

depreciation schedule in cells C74:H74 is given, as indicated above. Thus, for example, for year 1, the depreciation is $5,720 (=C74 × B73), and the depreciation tax savings for year 1 (cell C76) are $2,002 (= 5,720 × 0.35). This means PB saves $2,002 in taxes in year 1 by depreciating the equipment—depreciation is not an actual cash flow, but it impacts PB's cash flows by reducing its corporate income tax burden.

The complete analysis for PB is given in Table 6.6. If PB sells the machine, then it receives the revenue of $52,000 at the beginning of year 1 (alternatively, end of year 0). Revenues afterward consist of only selling the replacement parts to IU, which amounts to $2,000 per year in years 3–5. Total revenue is given in row 48. We then subtract the cost of goods sold (which is 55 percent of revenues, so for example, cell B49 is set to "=–0.55×B46"), yielding Earnings Before Tax (EBT), in row 50. Tax (row 51) is 35 percent of row 50, and that yields Net Income, in row 52. The NPV of the selling option (cell B53) is $16,412, given in Excel by the formula "=B52 + NPV(0.10, C52:G52)." Notice that in the selling option, the machine belongs to IU, and it is not in PB's balance sheet, so there is no depreciation expense for it.

The leasing option presents PB with revenues from leasing and maintenance payments from IU (rows 56 and 57, respectively). In addition, row 58 corresponds to the residual value of the machine to PB, which is $7,000 at the end of year 5. The sum of rows 56, 57, and 58 is given in row 59, total revenues. We then subtract the costs: COGS (again, at 55 percent of revenues) for the machine itself, and the maintenance cost, given in rows 60 and 61, respectively. Earnings Before Interest, Depreciation,

Table 6.6 PB lease versus buy analysis

	A	B	C	D	E	F	G	H
45	**Selling option**	Year 0	Year 1	Year 2	Year 3	Year 4	Year 5	
46	Revenue (machine)	$52,000						
47	Revenue (parts)	$ -	$ -	$ -	$2,000	$2,000	$2,000	
48	Total Revenue	$52,000	$ -	$ -	$2,000	$2,000	$2,000	
49	Less COGS	($28,600)	$ -	$ -	($1,100)	($1,100)	($1,100)	
50	EBT	$23,400	$ -	$ -	$900	$900	$900	
51	Tax	($8,190)	$ -	$ -	($315)	($315)	($315)	
52	Net Income	$15,210	$ -	$ -	$585	$585	$585	
53	NPV	$16,412						
54								
55	**Leasing option**		Year 1	Year 2	Year 3	Year 4	Year 5	Year 6
56	Lease payments	$ -	$12,000	$12,000	$12,000	$12,000	$12,000	
57	Maintenance payments	$ -	$2,200	$2,200	$2,200	$2,200	$2,200	
58	Residual value	$ -	$ -	$ -	$ -	$ -	$7,000	
59	Total revenues	$ -	$14,200	$14,200	$14,200	$14,200	$21,200	
60	COGS (year 0)	($28,600)	$ -	$ -	$ -	$ -	$ -	
61	Maintenance cost	$ -	($1,210)	($1,210)	($1,210)	($1,210)	($1,210)	
63	EBIDT	($28,600)	$12,990	$12,990	$12,990	$12,990	$19,990	
64	Tax	$ -	($4,547)	($4,547)	($4,547)	($4,547)	($6,997)	
65	Net Revenues	($28,600)	$8,444	$8,444	$8,444	$8,444	$12,994	
66	Tax savings (depreciation)	$ -	$2,002	$3,203	$1,922	$1,151	$1,151	$581
67	Net Income	($28,600)	$10,446	$11,647	$10,365	$9,595	$14,145	$581
68	NPV	$13,973						
69								
70	Preference for lease	($2,440)						

and Tax (EBIDT) is then given in row 63, as the sum of rows 59, 60, and 61. Because corporate income tax is calculated based on Earnings *after* incorporation of depreciation as an expense, but depreciation is not an actual cash flow, one can equivalently (from a purely cash flow perspective) calculate corporate tax (row 64) based on EBIDT (i.e., 35 percent of EBIDT), and then add back the tax savings from depreciation, from Table 6.5. Thus, row 65 (net revenues) is given by row 63 plus row 64. Note that there is no tax at year 0, as the product is depreciated (tax impact occurs in years 1–6). Row 66, tax savings from depreciation, is equal to row 76 from Table 6.5. Adding rows 65 and 66, we find the net income from the leasing option, which is row 67. The NPV of the leasing option (cell B68) is given by the formula "=B67 + NPV(0.10,C67:H67)," yielding $13,973. Comparing with cell B53, that provides a preference for lease for PB of ($2,440).

This analysis illustrates the fact that the lessor (PB) is in a higher corporate income tax bracket than the lessee (IU); this translates into tax savings of depreciation, which allows PB to pass these tax savings to IU in the form of low lease and maintenance payments. In addition, the salvage value of the used equipment to PB is higher than for IU, because PB can salvage parts and/or remanufacture the old equipment, whereas IU can only sell it in the secondary market to a broker.

CHAPTER 7

Closing the Loop— Remanufacturing

7.1 Scope of Remanufacturing in the United States and the World

Remanufacturing is the process of restoring a used product to a common esthetic and operating standard.[1] Broadly speaking, remanufacturing comprises the following steps: disassembly, cleaning, reworking, reassembly, and testing. Disassembly and reassembly are labor-intensive regardless of the product or industry. Cleaning is labor-intensive for most industries, and in automotive remanufacturing the process also takes a lot of capital and energy. Reworking is both labor- and capital-intensive. In automotive, tire, and industrial machinery remanufacturing, the process requires significant capital investments because it uses more advanced technology. Plus, products in these industries have a significant number of movable parts and are therefore more subject to mechanical wear and tear, implying a more comprehensive process (as opposed to, say, electronics, cartridges, and furniture).

An estimate of the size of remanufacturing in the United States from the United States International Trade Commission (USITC) is $43 billion, employing 180,000 people.[2] Perhaps due to the different terms, firms use to describe remanufactured products—such as "refurbished," "rebuilt," "reconditioned," "overhauled," and "restored"—it is difficult to pinpoint the largest remanufacturing industry. However, aerospace and automotive (including heavy-duty vehicles and parts) remanufacturing are among the largest, together accounting for at least half of all remanufacturing sales.[3] There also has been significant growth in information technology (IT) equipment and consumer electronics remanufacturing (such as in cell phones), likely because the fast pace of change in these industries has made available a large number of used products with significant value. For example, the U.S. market for remanufactured IT networking equipment has grown from a tiny figure in 2000 to over $2 billion in 2017, according to UNEDA, the trade association.[4]

Remanufacturing is mostly done by small, third-party firms. The USITC survey revealed that 2,900 firms with 20 or more employees perform remanufacturing in the United States. They also estimate 5,000 remanufacturing firms with fewer than 20 employees in the United States. While a number of original equipment manufacturers (OEMs), such as Hewlett-Packard, Dell, Ford, General Motors, Pitney Bowes, Bosch, and many others, offer remanufactured products, in many cases, these companies outsource the remanufacturing operations per se to other firms. The remanufacturers could be large, established companies (e.g., Solectron, Flex, Caterpillar) or small, independent third-party firms.

For small third-party firms, remanufacturing simply is a profitable proposition, as evidenced by the growth in the remanufacturing of printer cartridges. OEMs, on the other hand, typically see remanufacturing as an opportunity to expand their product line and offer a cheaper branded product to consumers who cannot or are not willing to pay the price for a new product. OEMs also offer their own remanufactured products as a way of protecting their brand, considering that most third-party remanufacturing firms follow their own quality standards when remanufacturing and that the brand may suffer if a third party offers a poor quality product that was originally manufactured by the OEM. Finally, remanufacturing may be the only option for unique products, those with low volume production, and those with long useful lives, such as defense items (e.g., weapons systems, fighter jets). However, OEMs may not engage in remanufacturing for fear of cannibalization of their product line, as we discuss later in this chapter.

An example of an OEM that remanufactures is Pitney Bowes, shown in Figure 7.1. Pitney Bowes is a Connecticut-based OEM that manufactures large-scale mailing equipment used in businesses. Pitney Bowes equipment matches customized documents to envelopes, weighs the parcel, prints postage, and sorts mail by ZIP code (a considerable source of savings given significant discounts offered by the U.S. Postal

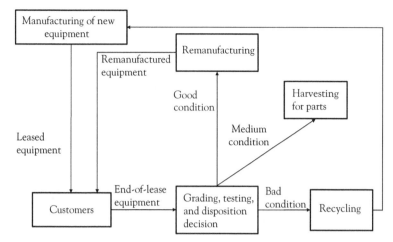

Figure 7.1 Closed-loop supply chain for Pitney Bowes.

Service for sorted mail). Pitney Bowes leases most of its new equipment, with a typical lease of four years. At the end of a lease, customers may upgrade to newer equipment if available. Used equipment is returned to Pitney Bowes, which evaluates the condition of the used machine and makes a disposition decision: recycling (done for the worst quality returns); dismantle for parts harvesting (done for medium quality returns), or remanufacturing (done for best quality returns). The remanufacturing process at Pitney Bowes includes total or partial disassembly, cleaning, replacement of consumable parts, cosmetic operations, upgrade of certain modules, and reassembly and testing. Remanufactured products are sold as a cheaper alternative to new products. The forward and reverse flows in a closed-loop supply chain (CLSC) impact each other: customers may opt for either remanufactured or new products, depending on their perception of qualities and prices for both products. The quantity of leased new products determines the availability of returns for remanufacturing in future years. As a result, management of a CLSC requires coordination between forward and reverse flows.

7.2   Product Acquisition

In regular manufacturing, the inputs—raw materials and components—are homogeneous. For example, two parts, with the same part number, supplied by the same supplier, are virtually identical. Sourcing parts from a certified supplier consists of ordering a given quantity of parts. In most cases, the quantity is at the manufacturer's discretion. The timing of arrival of these parts at the manufacturing plant can be predicted with a high degree of accuracy, as the order cycle time is usually known. In contrast, the inputs in remanufacturing—product returns, or cores—are heterogeneous in quality, quantity, and timing.

Particularly for end-of-use returns, the quality of returns is highly variable, depending on customer usage patterns and operating conditions. For example, an analysis of a sample of mailing equipment returned to Pitney Bowes in a given month, after a four-year lease, revealed the number of cycles (number of times the machine was used to run a job) to be between 200,000 and 1.6 million. Clearly, the amount of work, in labor and parts, necessary to restore these machines to a common esthetic and operating standard will vary significantly. In settings in which the quality of returns varies highly, firms need to implement a quality grading scheme. Incoming returns are graded according to a finite number of quality categories. This categorization is critical for planning capacity and managing the inventory of returns, particularly when returns exceed demand for remanufactured products and excess returns can be salvaged (for recycling or spare parts for example). Better quality returns have lower remanufacturing cost, consume less production capacity, and have higher salvage value. An academic study has concluded that five quality categories (e.g., worst, bad, medium, good, and best) are sufficient for deriving most of the benefits of quality grading.[5]

The uncertainty in timing and quantity of returns is mitigated when the firm leases most of its production, as is the case with Pitney Bowes, and can be minimized by implementing a *proactive acquisition strategy* that controls the incoming return stream. Such strategies include:

1. *Offering trade-in rebates.* Cummins offers a trade-in rebate for customers who buy a new diesel engine, if they return their old diesel engine. The trade-in rebate ensures a flow of returned diesel engines, which Cummins can remanufacture.

2. *Prepaid mailers.* Dell offers free collection and recycling of computers to residential customers upon the purchase of a new computer; this is done through a prepaid mailer.

3. *Higher prices for better quality returns.* Some cell phone remanufacturers control the quality of their return stream by offering higher prices for better quality returns.

7.3   Remarketing

Remanufactured products often are perceived to be inferior to new products. Researchers[6] auctioned identical new and remanufactured power tools on eBay and identical new and remanufactured Internet routers on eBay Business. The remanufactured and new products had identical manufacturer warranties. The researchers found that the winning bid—a measure of a consumer's willingness-to-pay—for the remanufactured product was 15 percent lower, on average, than the winning bid for the new product. Another study[7] found average price discounts for remanufactured products relative to new products ranging between 15 percent for some consumer electronics and 40 percent for video-game consoles at eBay; the remanufactured and new products had similar warranties. The large USITC survey[8] of American remanufacturers in diverse industries (such as compressors, automotive parts, office furniture, electrical motors, and industrial machinery) finds that remanufactured products command a 30–50 percent discount relative to comparable new products. Volkswagen remanufactured engines and parts in Europe command the same warranty as corresponding new engines and parts, at 24 months. Warranties for new and remanufactured products are about the same in the office furniture, power tool, and consumer electronics categories, even though the remanufactured products are cheaper by 40 percent, 15 percent, and 15–20 percent on average. Warranties for remanufactured toner cartridges can be as much as twice the length of new-cartridge warranties, although remanufactured cartridges are about 50 percent cheaper than new ones. Overall, it appears that, on average, the warranty period for remanufactured products is slightly shorter than that of new products. Shorter warranties only partially account for the price difference between new and remanufactured products. It appears that most of the price differences are better explained by consumer perception of remanufactured products.

Because of consumers' lower willingness-to-pay for remanufactured products, OEMs that remanufacture their product returns (e.g., HP,

Bosch, Pitney Bowes, and Cummins) price their remanufactured products at a lower point than new products. By doing so, they are able to expand their customer base by attracting customers who would not buy their new products because of the higher price. This is the *market expansion* effect. Still, price points (and corresponding warranties) must be chosen carefully to minimize the *cannibalization* effect, which is when customers who are willing to buy a (higher margin) new product buy a remanufactured product if it is priced significantly lower. To decrease cannibalization, many OEMs do not sell remanufactured products in the same channel as new products. For example, consumers cannot buy remanufactured HP computers at Best Buy. Instead, they must go to HP's online outlet store. Other OEMs, such as Cummins, offer remanufactured and new engines at the same dealers, because they believe the market expansion effect outweighs the cannibalization effect.

Some have argued for the existence of a *green segment*: consumers in this segment prefer a remanufactured product to a new one if they are in the same price range, although many consumers simply do not associate remanufactured products with green.[9] There is some evidence that some consumers prefer products with recycled content (but as seen before in Chapter 1, recycling and remanufacturing are distinct operations), as evidenced by the vibrant market for recycled office paper (even though recycled office paper costs about 6 percent more than virgin pulp paper due to the need for bleaching).

7.4   Industry Practice

Remanufacturing practice varies considerably from industry to industry. OEMs in some industries, such as manufacturers of printer cartridges, never offer remanufactured products because they fear cannibalization.

In other industries, such as the power tool industry, remanufactured products are seen by OEMs as an opportunity to expand their customer base and undercut competition from cheaper, non-brand name imports. As in the example of Pitney Bowes' mailing equipment, some industries have an abundance of product returns relative to demand for remanufactured products. For these industries, remanufacturing is constrained only by consumer demand, while in other industries, such as diesel engines, firms have to put incentives in place to collect the number of returns necessary to meet demand for remanufactured products.

These practices are discussed in more detail for four industries: cell phones and information technology (IT) networking equipment in Table 7.2, and automotive engines and cartridges in Table 7.1. These industries represent a range of products, from mostly mechanical (automotive engines) to mostly electronic (cell phones), as well as a range of remanufacturing processes, from very comprehensive (automotive engines) to faster and simpler (IT networking equipment). The information presented here was collected through plant visits and interviews with managers and from various online sources (e.g., websites of companies and trade associations and various online publications).

Remanufactured products can belong to the same technological generation as new products, or to an older generation. Same-generation technology can be found in industries where the technology does not evolve as quickly (e.g., retreaded tires for trucks), or when the product's useful life (sojourn time with the customer) is much lower than the product's lifecycle even if technology evolves quickly (e.g., toner cartridges). Finally, one can find same-generation remanufactured products, such as personal computers, smartphones, printers, and power tools, which originate from consumer returns. In many other cases, such as automotive engines, some Pitney Bowes equipment, medical equipment, and electrical motors, remanufactured, and new products may not belong to the same technological generation. In these cases, remanufacturing may provide some upgrades to the older technology, making the remanufactured product more appealing.

Consumers use remanufactured products as a natural substitute for comparable new products. However, as previously discussed, consumers rarely view remanufactured products as perfect substitutes for new ones. This perception of lower quality is reflected in the different pricing practices: remanufactured engines can be priced 40 percent lower than new engines; larger discounts can be found for older technology products such as some older IT networking equipment (discounts of as much as 95 percent). In general, the data in Tables 7.1 and 7.2 support the 30–50 percent discount range found on a larger-scale survey.[10]

Estimates of market size are based on the current sales by remanufacturers (e.g., $2 billion for information technology networking equipment)

Table 7.1 Remanufacturing practice in the automotive engine and printer cartridge industries

Dimension	Automotive engine remanufacturing	Cartridge remanufacturing
Technological generation	Remanufactured engines are typically of an older technological generation, but not necessarily.	Remanufactured and new cartridges are of the same technological generation.
Use of remanufactured products	Primarily by customers who cannot afford or do not want a new engine. Remanufactured engines have warranties between 1 and 3 years.	As a perfect substitute for new cartridges.
Pricing	Up to 40 percent cheaper than a new engine.	About 50 percent cheaper than a new cartridge.
Market Size	Approximately $2.5 billion in the United States (www.pera .org), although some managers indicate it is shrinking due to competition from cheaper imports.	Lyra Research (www.lyra.com) estimates between $100 million and $500 million, which is only 2–6 percent of the market for cartridges (the remainder comprises OEM new replacements and private brands).
Channels	Some OEMs offer remanufactured engines under a different brand (e.g., General Motors); others offer remanufactured and new engines in the same channel (e.g., Cummins).	Remanufacturers' websites. Some office-supply retailers (e.g., Office Depot) offer their own brand of remanufactured cartridges along with new OEM cartridges.
Source of returns	From dealers and brokers; typically from automobiles involved in accidents or engines that have reached their end of use, or through a trade-in program.	Customers return empty cartridges to remanufacturers (e.g., Laser-Tone) or retailers (e.g., Staples)
Acquisition cost	Varies significantly.	Low—mostly related to the logistic cost of placing collection bins and transportation, or prepaid mailers.
Remanufacturing cost	Between 40 percent and 65 percent less than the cost of manufacturing a new engine. Logistic costs (freight) are a key cost driver, making it not cost-effective to remanufacture in countries with low labor costs.	Up to 80 percent less than manufacturing a new cartridge.

Dimension	Automotive engine remanufacturing	Cartridge remanufacturing
Competitive landscape	Most OEMs (Ford, GM, Cummins, etc.) offer remanufactured engines; remanufacturing may be performed by the OEM itself (Cummins), or by other firms, such as Caterpillar and Jasper.	Large office-supply chains (Office Depot, Staples) are projected to dominate the market; the share of independent refillers is projected to decrease.
Reasons for OEM to remanufacture	To increase revenues, preempting third party remanufacturers, by offering a complement to their product line, an OEM-branded but cheaper remanufactured engine.	OEMs do not participate in the remanufactured cartridge market. OEMs actively attempt to shut down the market by melting older cartridges, adding chips in the product to disallow refilled cartridges from functioning, or limiting the number of refills.

Table 7.2 Remanufacturing in the cell phone and IT networking equipment industries

Dimension	Cell phone refurbishing	Information Technology (IT) networking equipment remanufacturing
Technological generation	Remanufactured and new products may or may not belong to the same technological generation.	Remanufactured and new products rarely belong to the same technological generation, with some exceptions (demo products, consumer returns).
Use of remanufactured Products	• For customers not willing to pay full price for a new phone. • As a replacement for warranty claims and for use during repairs. • In nonprofit organizations (e.g., shelters, emergency organizations) and developing countries.	Remanufactured products have much lower lead times and significant discounts. They are used in network expansion and redundancy, as a source of spare parts, and for training.
Pricing	Refurbished cell phones may command significant discounts (up to 50 percent off new).	Between 10 percent and 95 percent off an equivalent new product's price.

(*Continued*)

Table 7.2 Remanufacturing in the cell phone and IT networking equipment industries (Continued)

Dimension	Cell phone refurbishing	Information Technology (IT) networking equipment remanufacturing
Market size	About $14 billion worldwide, according to Gortner (http://www.gartner.com/newsroom/id/2986617).	Over $2 billion in the United States, according to the United Network Equipment Dealer Association (UNEDA; www.uneda.com).
Channels	Offered through third-party distribution centers or re-manufacturers' online stores.	Mostly online channels. Larger remanufacturers have dedicated sales forces.
Source of returns	Donations or customer upgrades to a new model. About 140 million phones are retired in the United States every year.	Technology upgrades, firms that go out of business, demo and training equipment.
Acquisition cost	Can be high ($140 per smartphone), due to significant market for second-hand phones.	Remanufacturers offer cash for trade. More popular products have market prices in an active secondary market.
Remanufacturing Cost	Depends significantly on the condition and type of used phone. Phones that cannot be remanufactured are recycled.	Between 5 percent and 20 percent of the cost of an equivalent new product.
Competitive Landscape	OEMs, trade-in firms, and many small firms, operating mostly locally.	Over 260 firms belong to UNEDA, the trade association
Reasons for OEM to Remanufacture	To increase market penetration into consumers with lower willingness-to-pay.	OEMs such as Cisco have a limited remanufacturing program (<1 percent of sales).

and do not indicate potential market size. Remanufactured products may gain more acceptance as consumers and buyers in general become more educated about their quality and performance levels compared with new products. Consumers' perception of quality may improve as industries consolidate, more rigorous standards for remanufacturing are adopted (typically through strong trade associations), and established players emerge in other industries. In fact, there is strong empirical evidence that a remanufacturer's reputation plays a strong role in the buyer's willingness to purchase remanufactured consumer products.[11] Another favorable trend for remanufacturing is the increase in leasing and "pay-for-service" practices, where consumers buy a service rather than a product. For example, in the commercial retreaded tire industry, large fleet operators have contracts with tire shops (who are often retreaders) to provide good tires for a certain number of miles. Whether the shop uses retreaded or new tires is not of concern to the fleet operator. Similarly, Xerox offers services where customers pay for the number of pages printed.

Remanufactured and new products may be distributed through the same channel as new products—that is the case with automotive engines remanufactured by major OEMs such as Ford, General Motors and Cummins, Caterpillar's equipment sold at its dealer network, or remanufactured toner cartridges in large office-supply chains such as Staples. In many cases, remanufactured products are distributed separately, in outlets or online stores, due to fear of cannibalization. This was clear in interactions with managers of consumer electronics and business-to-business IT equipment firms. Across a sample of 274 remanufacturers in diverse industries, a study found that 64 percent of remanufactured products were sold directly to the user. Only 15 percent were sold through retailers and distributors.[12]

Returns (or cores) are the main input to remanufacturing, and they may come from a variety of sources. In the toner cartridge industry, consumers (or businesses) mail old cartridges to remanufacturers to be refilled. The firm mails back in-stock remanufactured cartridges. Ford collects cores from 4,000 dealers, using the same third-party logistics company that distributes new engines (through milk-runs). Cores are shipped to a location where they are evaluated for quality; bad quality cores are disposed of and good cores are kept in a warehouse for future remanufacturing. Ford maintains several months' worth of inventory of cores to accommodate long remanufacturing lead times and ensure that the remanufacturing operation is not halted because of a lack of cores. Consumer returns are a natural source of returns for remanufacturing for firms selling to consumers (as opposed to businesses) such as Hewlett-Packard, Dell, and Bosch. The cost of collection and transportation can be a significant cost driver for acquisition in such industries as automotive engines and large and heavy equipment.

Remanufacturing cost is a fraction of the cost of manufacturing a new product. Our experiences with many firms indicate that this cost ranges between 5 percent and 40 percent of the cost of a new product.

However, some managers in industries where remanufacturing is labor intensive and technology is complex (e.g., automotive engines) indicated that remanufacturing cost is rising compared with cheaper imports.

For firms considering remanufacturing—whether an OEM or a third party—industry structure (i.e., concentration, number of players) as well as the dynamics of competition between remanufactured and new products are significant factors. As discussed previously, a reason for OEMs to remanufacture is to expand their customer base by reaching a customer segment that cannot afford or is not willing to pay the (higher) price for a new product. By offering a cheaper remanufactured alternative, OEMs also drive away some of the competition from third parties. This reasoning is clear in the automotive engine industry, where most OEMs offer remanufactured engines in addition to new ones. Caterpillar also offers remanufactured equipment side by side with new equipment. It is also in the interest of the OEM to offer remanufactured products from consumer returns, due to the significant potential for value recovery and the relatively lower volume, which outweighs cannibalization concerns. The cannibalization threat, however, can be significant to the point that OEMs refuse to engage in remanufacturing (or do it to a limited extent), as seen in our discussion of toner cartridges, cell phones, and information technology networking equipment. In the tire retreading industry, OEMs develop the retreading technology and license it to other shops, in essence outsourcing the remanufacturing. It is common for the OEMs to outsource the remanufacturing process to certified third parties, as do Ford, Hewlett-Packard, Pitney Bowes, and many others. Most remanufacturing industries are fragmented, with a large number of smaller players, as discussed in the introduction.

7.5 Strategic, Tactical, and Operational Issues in Remanufacturing

For managers considering engaging in remanufacturing—whether as third-party firms or OEMs—there are a number of strategic, operational, and tactical issues to consider:

- *Strategic.* How should the reverse supply chain be designed? Specifically, where are the locations of collection, consolidation, remanufacturing, and recycling sites? Should an OEM remanufacture? If so, what should be the prices and corresponding warranties for remanufactured products? Should the firm lease or sell its products? Should an OEM (over) design certain components of a product so that these components' parts can be reused for remanufacturing in the future? If so, which components should be reused and which components should be replaced with new components upon remanufacturing?

- *Tactical.* Product acquisition for remanufacturing: How many returns should be procured, at which quality level, and at which price? Production planning for remanufacturing: How many returns of each type (quality grade) should be remanufactured and disposed of in each period? How many returns should be kept in stock for future use?

- *Operational.* How should the different remanufacturing operations be scheduled at the shop? Disassembly planning: What is the sequence and depth of disassembly?

The reader interested in some of the issues in more detail is referred to Ferguson and Souza.[13]

7.6   Web Resources

- RIT Center for Remanufacturing: http://www.reman.rit.edu/gis/remanufacturing
- Remanufacturing Industries Council: http://www.remancouncil .org/
- Automotive Parts Remanufacturers Association: http://www.apra .org/
- USITC Report: https://www.usitc.gov/publications/332/pub4356 .pdf

CHAPTER 8

Sustainability in the Supply Chain

8.1   Selling Green Products: Environmental Product Differentiation

Environmental product differentiation refers to the idea of designing and marketing products that provide a lower environmental impact than competing products of similar functionality. Designing and manufacturing "green" products typically (but not always) increase a firm's production costs, as discussed in Chapter 5; for example, the firm needs to use higher quality materials that can be upcycled at the end of a product's use with consumers. As a result, for a green product to be economically sustainable to the firm marketing it, it needs to:

1. Increase the firm's market share by attracting new customers who find the "green" attribute appealing, and/or
2. Command a price premium

Thus, the firm needs to differentiate the "green" product along environmental lines. Following established principles of strategic management, Forest Reinhardt suggests three requirements for a successful environmental product differentiation strategy, and they are outlined in Table 8.1.[1] Although the requirements in Table 8.1 were originally developed considering environmental product differentiation, they are equally valid for the purposes of differentiating a product along socially responsible, or ethical lines (i.e., the other "P" of sustainability—people). Understanding these principles is important not only for firms attempting to design and

Table 8.1 Requirements for successful environmental (or ethical) product differentiation[2]

Number	Requirement
1	Create or *find a willingness to pay* (WTP) among customers for environmental (or ethical) quality
2	Establish *credible information* about the product's green (or ethical) attributes
3	The "green" (or ethical) innovation must be *defensible against imitation* by competitors.

market green (or ethical) products, but also for firms who buy green (or ethical) products from suppliers (such as is the case with Walmart or other retailers). We therefore comment on these requirements in detail now.

8.2   Requirement 1: Create or Find a Willingness to Pay (WTP) Among Customers for Environmental (or Ethical) Quality

Industrial Markets

In industrial markets, a firm can increase the customer's WTP for its green product under two scenarios:

- *Reduction in total cost of ownership for the product.* Industrial buyers are sophisticated, and therefore consider the total cost of ownership, throughout the product's life cycle, when making a purchasing decision. As discussed in Chapter 6, Interface is a manufacturer of modular carpet tiles, which can be replaced selectively (e.g., a customer may replace tiles in high traffic areas more frequently). Interface has also developed a proprietary recycling technology—ReEntry 2.0—allowing carpet materials (nylon facing, and PVC backing) to be upcycled. Interface is a firm that promotes its environmentally friendly practices in carpet design, manufacturing, and end-of-life, and it can thus increase a customer's WTP for its modular, greener carpet, if the design actually reduces the total cost of ownership for the customer. This can be accomplished through an operating leasing program, where Interface owns the carpet, and recovers the carpet at the end of the leasing period. The recovered carpet is valuable to Interface as a source of raw materials (considering its recycling program), and if there are additional tax benefits (such as those discussed in Chapter 6, related to depreciation tax savings), then Interface can reduce the leasing payments, and make it more attractive to the customer.

- *Reduction in regulatory compliance risks*: If there is the risk of future environmental regulation related to a dimension impacted by the green product, the green product has the potential to reduce future compliance costs. For example, the European Union (EU) has set a target of 20 percent for the proportion of electricity derived from renewable sources (such as wind, solar, hydroelectric, and geothermal) for each of the member states by 2020. This high-level requirement (at the country level) may trickle down to firms, if a country in the EU passes legislation regulating electricity consumption at the customer level. Thus, a large retailer may find it attractive to install solar panels at its stores (with a high initial investment cost) rather than purchasing electricity from regular sources, in order to reduce potential future compliance costs.

Consumer Markets

Firms may find consumer segments that are willing to pay a premium for the green attributes of the product:

- *Selling to "altruistic" consumers.* These would be consumers who are willing to pay a higher price for a product because this is the "right thing to do." Examples include consumers of Fairtrade products, as documented in the case about Nestlé's introduction of Fairtrade coffee in the instant coffee segment in the UK.[3] Fairtrade is a certification provided by the Fairtrade Labelling Organization and its affiliates that ensures that certified products have their agricultural raw materials—coffee beans in this case—comply with certain standards, for example, farmers are paid minimum prices (i.e., they are not paid according to prevailing commodity market prices, which fluctuate according to supply and demand), and/or certain ethical conditions are met. Nestlé's marketing department had documented three segments of consumers with respect to the "ethical product" category: "Global Watchdogs," "Conscientious Consumers," and "Do What I cans." Consumers in the first two segments were targets for the introduction of an instant coffee that was Fairtrade certified, despite its price premium.

- *Green (or ethical) product provides a "health" appeal.* This is evidenced by the growth of organic food sales: organic food and beverage sales in the United States have grown from $1 billion in 1990 to $47 billion in 2016, with a growth rate of 8.8 percent from 2015 to 2016.[4] As another example, Walmart's consumers—who are likely to be more price sensitive—are apparently willing to pay a premium for clothes made with organic cotton (due to the overall feel and quality of the product, in addition to its health appeal), considering that some of these products sell at a premium.

- *Products make a statement to friends and acquaintances.* Products that are highly visible when being consumed may provide some consumers with the recognition they want for being "cool." For example, the Toyota Prius had a distinct design, which made it easily recognized. This feature is appealing to some consumers who want to advertise to others (friends and/acquaintances) that they are concerned about the environment, considering the vehicle's advertised green qualities. (This is in direct contrast with, e.g., the Toyota Camry hybrid, which looked just like the regular gas-only Camry).

8.3   Establish Credible Information about the Product's Green (or Ethical) Attributes

This is more easily accomplished through government, or third-party certification (of the product's green and/or ethical attributes) that is credible. Self-Certification initiatives are problematic because customers do not have a mechanism to directly assess the firm's environmental friendliness claims. In addition, some firms may advertise a product's environmental qualities for a single stage of its life cycle, such as during consumer use. As we have been stressing in this book, a product's environmental impact must be assessed using such tools as Life-cycle Assessment (LCA), where a product's environmental impact is measured and added across all stages of the product's life cycle: raw material extraction, transportation, manufacturing, packaging, distribution, use by consumers, and end of life. For example, many hybrid and electric car manufacturers stress in their marketing initiatives that those products are more environmentally friendly than vehicles with regular internal combustion engines. That is certainly true if one considers energy consumption (and consequently global warming potential) during the product's use by consumers. Hybrid and electric cars, however, by design contain a significant amount of batteries, and the environmental impact of those batteries—either at the end of their life (i.e., recycling potential)—or regarding materials choice (toxicity, depletion levels, etc.) must be assessed, among other dimensions, for a complete picture.

Products can be certified through government-sponsored labels, or third-party certifications. We discuss some examples of each type now.

Government-Sponsored Labels

There are several examples of government-sponsored labels:

Energy Star

This is a symbol backed by the U.S. Environmental Protection Agency (EPA) that can be displayed on energy-efficient products (and buildings). The EPA has some guiding principles when awarding a product the right to display the symbol.[5]

- The product category must contribute significant energy savings: larger appliances (such as refrigerators, dishwashers, water coolers, and washers), building products (such as insulation, roofing, windows, and doors), heating and cooling, lighting and fans, and water heaters.
- Products must deliver similar performance to comparable products, in addition to being more energy-efficient.
- Customers should be able to recover their initial investment— if the Energy Star certified product costs more initially than a

comparable non-Energy Star product—through lower utility bills, in a reasonable period of time.

- Product energy consumption and performance can be measured and verified with testing.
- Products must display the Energy Star label visibly to consumers, to differentiate from other products.

SmartWay

SmartWay is a collaboration between the U.S. EPA and the freight transportation industry, targeted at improving fuel efficiency in that industry. The SmartWay program has three components[6]:

- *SmartWay Transport Partnership.* Here carriers, logistics companies, freight shippers, multimodal carriers, and rail carriers agree to calculate and track their fuel consumption and carbon footprint annually. In exchange, EPA ranks and publicizes each firm's performance in the SmartWay Partner list. Best performers have the right to exhibit the SmartWay partner logo.
- *SmartWay Brand.* This program develops test protocols, and verifies performance of vehicles, and other technologies with the potential to reduce greenhouse gases from freight transport. Example of technologies tested and certified here include idle reduction technologies (such as electrified parking spaces, auxiliary power units, thermal storage system, among others), aerodynamic technologies (such as trailer gap reducers, trailer side skirts, and trailer boat tails, among others), low-rolling resistance tires, and verified retrofit technologies (such as diesel oxidation catalysts, and diesel particulate filters). Best performers can display the SmartWay brand, helping to accelerate availability, adoption, and market penetration of fuel saving technologies.
- *SmartWay Global Collaboration.* This program provides guidance and resources for other countries that want to implement programs similar to SmartWay. It also works with organizations to harmonize sustainability accounting methods in the freight sector.

USDA Organic

The United States Department of Agriculture (USDA) National Organic Program provides standards and regulations that certify organic products sold by a firm, wild crop harvesting, or handling operation. Broadly speaking, organic operations should be able to demonstrate that they are "protecting natural resources, conserving biodiversity, and using only approved substances."[7] There are accredited certifying agents in many states in the United States, as well as more than 20 countries on all five continents. A brief summary of the requirements for USDA organic labeling is provided in the USDA website, and reproduced below[8]:

- *Organic crops.* The USDA organic seal verifies that irradiation, sewage sludge, synthetic fertilizers, prohibited pesticides, and genetically modified organisms were not used.
- *Organic livestock.* The USDA organic seal verifies that producers meet animal health and welfare standards, did not use antibiotics or growth hormones, used 100 percent organic feed, and provided animals with access to the outdoors.
- *Organic multi-ingredient food.* The USDA organic seal verifies that the product has 95 percent or more certified organic content. If the label claims that it was made with specified organic ingredients, you can be sure that those specific ingredients are certified organic.

RoHS (Restriction on the Use of Certain Hazardous substances)

This is actually a directive (regulation) introduced by the European Union (EU) in 2003, and in effect since 2006; it became law in all EU member states. The directive restricts the use of six substances—lead (Pb), mercury (Hg), cadmium (Cd), hexavalent chromium (Cr^{6+}), polybrominated biphenyls (PBB), and polybrominated diphenyl ether (PDBE)—in electric and electronic products, as defined by the WEEE directive (see Chapter 2). PBB and PDBE are flame retardants used in several plastics. The maximum concentration allowed for these substances is 0.1 percent (except for Cd, whose maximum allowed concentration is 0.01 percent) by weight of homogeneous material (i.e., any substance in the product that can be separated mechanically). Products must exhibit the RoHS label.

Even though RoHS is law in Europe, some retailers in the United States (such as Walmart) adopted a policy of buying only RoHS-compliant electronic products such as TVs, computers, audio products, and phones.[9]

Dolphin Safe Tuna

The U.S. Department of Commerce sponsors a label that certifies that tuna caught in the eastern tropical Pacific Ocean—where tuna and dolphins are closely associated—preserves and protects dolphin stocks. The certification is accomplished through systematic audits, as well as through spot checks. There are, however, other dolphin safe labels provided by third-party agencies, such as the Earth Island Institute. According to the Earth Island Institute, over 95 percent of the world's tuna canners are dolphin safe.[10] Thus, this particular certification is not really a differentiator in the market place, but rather a requirement.

Third-party Certifications

There are numerous third-party certifications for a product's green attributes. We provide some well recognized examples below, but of course, this list is far from exhaustive.

Marine Stewardship Council (MSC)

MSC is a non-governmental organization (NGO) that sets standards for sustainable fishing, which was established by Unilever and the World Wildlife Fund (WWF). Due to overfishing, a study in the journal *Science* pointed out that *all* species of wild seafood are severely depleted and predicted a collapse of worldwide fisheries by 2048.[11] There is thus an increased interest in and attention on sustainable fishing practices. As of May of 2017, there were 286 certified fisheries in the MSC program, all over the world. To be certified, a fishery must comply with the MSC environmental standard for sustainable fishing. In a nutshell, the MSC environmental standard for sustainable fishing is built on three principles[12]:

- *Principle 1.* Sustainable fish stocks: The fishing activity must be at a level that is sustainable for the fish population. Any certified fishery must operate so that fishing can continue indefinitely and is not overexploiting the resources.

- *Principle 2.* Minimizing environmental impact: Fishing operations should be managed to maintain the structure, productivity, function, and diversity of the ecosystem on which the fishery depends.
- *Principle 3.* Effective management: The fishery must meet all local, national, and international laws and must have a management system in place to respond to changing circumstances and maintain sustainability.

The principles above are supported by detailed criteria, available at the MSC website.[13] Once a fishery has been certified, all companies in the supply chain—from boat, to the restaurant or retailer that wants to sell MSC certified seafood—must have the MSC Chain of Custody Certification, and apply the corresponding ecolabel. To obtain the MSC Chain of Custody Certification[14]:

> The MSC Chain of Custody Standard is a traceability and segregation standard that is applicable to the full supply chain from a certified fishery or farm to final sale. Each company in the supply chain handling or selling an MSC certified product must have a valid MSC Chain of Custody certificate. This assures consumers and seafood-buyers that MSC labeled seafood comes from a certified sustainable fishery.

As a component of its sustainability strategy, Walmart has committed to purchasing 100 percent of its wild seafood from MSC certified suppliers, and the company is close to achieving that goal in the United States, at 90 percent. Because of decreasing output in world fisheries as discussed before, a key benefit to Walmart of obtaining MSC-certified seafood is continuity of supply, considering the firm's large purchasing volumes worldwide.

Forest Stewardship Council (FSC)

FSC is an NGO that was established in 1993 in response to concerns over deforestation globally. Similar to MSC, FSC provides three types of certification: Forest Management, Chain of Custody, and FSC Controlled Wood. Forest Management Certification must meet specific requirements that are derived from 10 basic principles, which can be summarized as follows[15]:

- Legality Verification—follow all applicable laws
- Demonstrated long-term land tenure and use rights
- Respect rights of workers, indigenous peoples
- Equitable use and sharing of benefits
- Reduction of environmental impact of logging activities
- Identification and appropriate management of areas that need special protection (e.g., cultural or sacred sites, habitat of endangered animals or plants).

The Chain of Custody Certification ensures that forest products can be traced back to the producer, and is targeted at firms that manufacture, process, or trade in forest products (such as timber). The FSC Controlled Wood Certification allows manufacturers to mix FSC-certified wood with non-certified wood, and then apply a MIX FSC label. The non-certified wood, however, must comply with the FSC Controlled Wood standards, which specify that the following five origins must be avoided[16]:

1. Illegally harvested wood
2. Wood harvested in violation of traditional and civil rights
3. Wood harvested in forests in which high conservation values (areas particularly worth of protection) are threatened through management activities
4. Wood harvested from conversion of natural forests
5. Wood harvested from areas where genetically modified trees are planted

FSC sets the standards, but the Certification itself is performed by independent Certification bodies. FSC is well recognized. For example, a building can obtain one point (MR Credit: Building Product Disclosure and Optimization—Sourcing of Raw Materials) toward LEED Certification (see Chapter 4), if it uses a minimum of 25 percent (based on cost) of

FSC-certified products for wood building components, such as structural framing, flooring, doors, and finishes. There are, however, other competing ecolabels for wood such as the Sustainable Forestry Initiative, and the Rainforest Alliance.

Fairtrade

As discussed earlier in this chapter, Fairtrade is a Certification provided by the Fairtrade Labelling Organization and its affiliates that ensures that certified products have their agricultural raw materials (e.g., coffee beans, cotton, fruit, bananas, rice, tea, fresh fruit, among others) comply with certain standards. For example, producers (farmers) must be paid minimum prices (instead of fluctuating commodity market prices), and/ or certain ethical conditions must be met. In addition, producers must be paid an additional sum—the Fairtrade Premium—to invest in their communities.[17]

LEED (Leadership in Energy and Environmental Design)

LEED is a rating system for buildings created by the U.S. Green Building Council (USGBC), and it was discussed previously in Chapter 4. Although a building is not a consumer or industrial product, a firm may use its achievements in LEED certified buildings (say, its headquarters, factories, or warehouses) to boost its green image among consumers.

Cradle-to-Cradle

This is a Certification provided by McDonough Braungart Design Chemistry (MBDC) for products designed according to cradle-to-cradle principles. These principles were discussed in detail in Chapter 5, and can be summarized as follows: (i) product components must be homogeneous in terms of materials (i.e., made of either biological materials, which can be composted, such as wood and cotton; or technical materials, which can be upcycled, such as aluminum and some plastics), (ii) all materials in the product must satisfy non-toxicity requirements, and (iii) the product must have a minimum material reutilization score, which is derived from the percentage of recycled materials, as well as the percentage of recyclable materials. Products certified at the silver, gold, and platinum levels should meet additional criteria, in terms of renewable energy use, water steward-ship, and social responsibility. As discussed before, the set of criteria for certification are quite stringent, and to date relatively few complex prod-ucts have been cradle-to-cradle certified.

The list above is just a sample of well-known green labels; a list that grows quickly every year. But the key point is that a firm can establish credible information about its product's green attributes by pursuing a credible third-party (government or not) certification, and reputable ecolabels provide just that. Self-reported, difficult to validate and verify claims of greenness can easily backfire, and firms should understand the perils of greenwashing.

8.4   Requirement 3: Barriers to Imitation

For successful differentiation along environmental lines, the product's environmental attributes must be difficult to imitate. Examples of barriers to imitation include:

- *Patent protection.* If processes or technologies can be patented, they provide a natural barrier to imitation. Examples here abound, as firms usually pursue patent protection for technologies developed in-house.

- *Unpatentable but proprietary capabilities.* Some capabilities are not really patentable, but they may nonetheless be difficult to replicate. For example, Benziger is a California winery known for its biody-namic vineyards, which are self-regulating systems that go beyond organic agriculture. Biodynamic vineyards function according to closed natural cycles. For example, water used in wine production is completely purified through a natural system of ponds and living organisms. As another example, the vineyard has a patch of plants that attracts "good bugs," which then prey on the "bad bugs," elim-inating the need for pesticides. Weeds are controlled via a flock of sheep. The integrated set of such biodynamic agricultural practices is a capability that is difficult to replicate, at least in the short term.

- *First mover advantage.* First movers (i.e., early adopters of green technologies) enjoy the reputation effects of being first, as well as being further down the learning curve. As an example Sanofi Genzyme's headquarters (Sanofi Genzyme is the specialty care global business unit of Sanofi, specializing in therapies for rare diseases, multiple sclerosis, oncology, and immunology) was the largest corporate office building to earn the Platinum LEED Certification, and one of only 13 buildings ever to receive this rating, at the time of the Certification in 2005. Many auto executives attribute Toyota's reputation as a green auto manufacturer to Toyota Prius, which was the first successful hybrid vehicle.

- *An integrated approach to environmental issues.* Some firms have developed a green reputation over time, a result of years of programs and practices designed to minimize their environmental impact. Examples here include Patagonia in apparel, Steelcase and Herman Miller in office furniture, and Interface in carpeting. Reputation is difficult to imitate.

The three principles of environmental product differentiation detailed above provide some guidance to firms seeking to establish their green credentials, both in terms of their own products and services, and from their supply chains. In fact, some ecolabels (such as FSC, MSC, and Fairtrade) have chain of custody requirements as detailed above, which calls for an integrated supply chain approach. This is not surprising because firms are linked by complex, global supply chains, and sustainability actions by one firm in the chain have a direct impact on other firms in that chain.

8.5   Web Resources

The following websites provide more in-depth information about the requirements for earning some of the green labels discussed in this chapter:

- U.S. EPA Energy Star: http://www.energystar.gov/
- U.S. EPA Smartway: http://www.epa.gov/smartway
- USDA organic: http://www.ams.usda.gov, Natural Organic Program
- MSC Certification: http://www.msc.org/
- FSC Certification: http://www.fsc.org/
- Fairtrade Certification: http://www.fairtrade.net/
- Cradle-to-Cradle design Certification: http://www.mbdc.com/

CHAPTER 9

The Other "P" of Sustainability—People

9.1 Introduction

Much of the emphasis of the book is on two of the Ps of sustainability: profit and planet. This chapter is dedicated to the other "P" of sustainability: people. We discuss some examples of firms that have considered their *social* impact when designing their operations and supply chains.

In general, when a firm considers the environmental impacts of their operations, they are also considering the social impact, although perhaps indirectly:

- *Pollution prevention and waste reduction.* A firm that pollutes less is contributing to the better health of the citizens in the communities where it operates. For example, lower emissions of SO_2 decrease the intensity of acid rains, which protects the health of plants and animals, which indirectly impacts human health through better food supply and a better quality of life. Reducing or eliminating the waste streams that contaminate a community's water supply directly improves the health of its citizens. In general, reducing the amount of waste also means reducing the rate of landfilling. Landfilling has a direct negative impact on the health of humans, because some toxic materials may leak and contaminate water streams.

- *Carbon footprint reduction.* When a firm reduces its carbon footprint, it is contributing to reducing the intensity of global warming. Although global warming may be beneficial to some communities (e.g., longer growing season in cold areas of Canada), its potential negative impacts are stronger in a larger portion of planet, including poorer communities in tropical areas of the world. That is because impacts of global warming include rising sea levels, a change in the amount and pattern of precipitation, and a likely expansion of subtropical deserts.[1] According to the Intergovernmental Panel on Climate Change (IPCC), the direct negative impacts of global warming on humans include vulnerability to extreme weather events (such as hurricanes, and droughts), as well as coastal flooding, reduction in water supplies, and reduction in food supplies (due to droughts and floods).[2]

- *Green buildings*. As discussed in Chapter 4, one of the strongest impacts of green buildings on humans (in addition to lower environmental impact) is increased employee productivity (working in a healthier environment, with better temperature, ventilation, indoor air quality, and natural illumination), estimated to be around 5 percent.

- *Design for the environment (DfE)*. The link is direct here, if one considers that DfE protocols emphasize materials choice, and that includes an assessment of toxicity to humans. For example, the cradle-to-cradle design Certification discussed in Chapter 5 (in the section "Cradle-to-Cradle® Design Principles") specifically bans the use of PVC and chloroprene at any concentrations on product designs, and sets very low limits for the use of halogenated hydrocarbon and toxic heavy metals (Pb, Hg, Cd, Cr^{+6}). A product that is non-toxic has a direct positive impact on consumers' health.

The list above is not meant to be exhaustive, but it provides examples where the lower environmental impact of a firm's operations has direct and indirect positive impacts on the health of humans, and their quality of life. This shows how the "planet P" is related to the "people P." In this chapter, however, we provide examples where firms design their operations and supply chains taking into consideration more direct social impacts, and how they can gain a competitive advantage through shared value creation.

9.2   Stakeholder Analysis

In order to understand the reach of a firm's social impact, one needs to understand the various stakeholders of a firm:

- *Employees.* Firms provide direct and indirect employment, and that is a direct positive impact on communities. For example, General Motors (GM) employs 225,000 people in more than 120 countries.[3] In terms of indirect employment, there are GM's suppliers, and all the services that exist around GM plants and suppliers to support the employees, such as restaurants, health-care services, hotels, and so forth. Of course, employment is only one indicator of social impact related to employees. Working conditions, benefits (including health insurance), diversity practices, and so forth also need to be considered.

- *Communities.* Firms have a direct impact in the communities where they operate. As previously discussed, they provide direct and indirect employment. But they can also support local schools, hospitals, local charities, cultural events, environmental initiatives, and in many cases these are win–win partnerships. In some cases, this support can be classified as philanthropy, or charity. For example, Lilly, the pharmaceutical company headquartered in Indianapolis, Indiana, has several initiatives aimed at improving access to health care for underserved populations. Among its many initiatives, Lilly donates medications to several, patient assistance programs in the United States and abroad. Some less-developed countries may gain access to licenses for making Lilly's patent-protected drugs, so that drug manufacturers may make generic versions of Lilly's patent-protected drugs at a much lower cost. As another example, Johnson & Johnson (J&J), which manufactures drugs and medical and diagnosis devices, among other products, lists several social responsibilities initiatives on its website.[4] One initiative provides training for midwives to assist in births, with impact estimated at six million births by 2020. As another example, J&J provides HIV medicines either at special effort or at reduced pricing in more than 100 countries. J&J donates medication to several NGOs around the world, for example, 129 million doses of mebendazole in 2015 for treatment of children with worms in countries in Africa, Asia, and Central America. In other cases, community support is a win–win, or shared value creation, as we discuss later in this chapter. For example, strong local schools help provide a quality workforce, and also improve the local quality of life, increasing employee retention.

- *Customers*. Firms can have a significant social impact in their customers by developing products that help save lives and improve quality of life. Consider, for example, the pharmaceutical companies previously described, and their impact on their customers' health, and global health in general. As another example of a product designed to meet societal problems, Procter & Gamble (P&G) has developed water purifying packets for use in poor areas of the world or in natural disasters, where water sanitation is an issue. One small P&G packet turns 10 liters of dirty, potentially deadly water into clear, drinkable water. P&G's Children's Safe Drinking Water Program works with several partners to provide the water purification packets to schools, health clinics, and disasters such as cholera outbreaks, earth quakes, and floods. By 2015, the program had delivered 9 billion liters of clean water to those in need, and had a goal of 15 billion liters to be delivered in 2020.[5]

- *Supplier*. Firms can have a positive impact in their suppliers, by offering training, financing, and support. These are examples of win–win situations, in that supplier development improves sourcing in the long run, reducing costs and improving quality. For example, consider Walmart's efforts in securing MSC-certified seafood previously described. Such developments help economic sustainability of the firm in terms of assurance of quality supply. There are also examples of direct social support of suppliers, for example, Nestlé's training and technical assistance to 113,446 coffee farmers in 2016.[6] This improves profitability of the farmers, and helps Nestlé secure a long-term supply of coffee.

- *Non-governmental organizations (NGOs).* Although some NGOs have a combative tone with firms, many firms and NGOs have realized that, instead, a collaborative approach yields dividends for both parties. Continuing on the coffee example, Nestlé has not only its own farmer support initiatives, but it also sells Fairtrade-certified coffee, as discussed in Chapter 8. Tetra Pak is a multi-national headquartered in Switzerland that manufactures, among other products, long-life packaging—cartons manufactured with aseptic technology, which keeps food (such as milk and juices) fresh for at least six months without refrigeration or preservatives. Tetra Pak's packages are complex, with six different layers of three materials: paper, polyethylene terephthalate (PET), and aluminum. Tetra Pak has engaged with numerous NGOs around the world, such as the Forest Stewardship Council (FSC) since a key raw material is paper, the World Resource Institute (WRI) for carbon and water footprint accounting, and many others, including those with a more social bend, such as Scaling Up Nutrition.[7]

- *Industry Groups.* Continuing with the Tetra Pak example, the firm is engaged with several industry groups, such as Carton Council, to promote standards for recyclable packages, as well as increasing recycling rates.

- *Governments.* Firms, particularly large OEMs, have an interest in keeping a good relationship with governments, either local or national governments. As discussed in Chapter 4, good relationships with local governments may ease the issuance of permits, and enhance license to operate in general. National government agencies are the source of regulations, and national legislation, and thus firms can successfully lobby for the establishment and improvement of these regulations. For example, the European Recycling Platform (ERP) has successfully lobbied the European Union for the establishment of the WEEE directive for e-waste recycling, which is based on the principle of individual producer responsibility, as discussed in Chapter 2. Again, this is a win–win situation, as firms can improve their competitive position, and governments can improve environmental and social welfare through better, more informed legislation and regulations.

9.3   Shared Value

Some of the examples in the previous section on stakeholder analysis, and in this book in general, illustrate the idea of **shared value**. As Porter and Kramer define[8]:

> The concept of shared value can be defined as policies and operating practices that enhance the competitiveness of a company while simultaneously advancing the economic and social conditions in the communities in which it operates. Shared value creation focuses on identifying and expanding the connections between societal and economic progress.

Or, as the Shared Value Initiative puts it[9]:

> Shared value is a management strategy in which companies find business opportunities in social problems. While philanthropy and CSR [Corporate Social Responsibility] focus efforts on "giving back" or minimizing the harm business has on society, shared value focuses company leaders on maximizing the competitive value of solving social problems in new customers and markets, cost savings, talent retention, and more.

Notice the direct contrast between the idea of CSR and shared value in the two quotes. Porter and Kramer suggest seven main areas where addressing societal concerns can lead to higher productivity; these arguments are in line with what has been presented in this book:

1. *Environmental impact.* By now it should be clear to the reader that when a firm significantly reduces its environmental impact, it enjoys many productivity benefits, in line with the lean philosophy of reducing waste. Consider the previous TetraPak example, where increased recycling rates of its packages lead to both lower environmental impact and cost reductions in the form of lower raw material costs.

2. *Energy use.* Reducing energy use, or, more succinctly, a firm's carbon footprint, directly contributes to the bottom line, as articulated many times in this book.

3. *Water use.* Again, solid water stewardship implies lower costs in the short run, and it also ensures water supply in the long run. Coca-Cola, for example, has invested heavily in understanding water scarcity and abundance around the world, in reducing its own water efficiency and footprint, and making sure that all water used in their facilities are returned to a level that supports aquatic life, even when not required by local governments.[10] In terms of water efficiency, for example, Coca-Cola has a goal to improve water efficiency by 25 percent by 2020, compared to a 2010 baseline.[11]

4. *Employee health.* Investing in a wellness program means lower absenteeism and higher morale; all contributing to higher productivity.

5. *Employee skills.* Similarly, improving employee skills through training programs such as tuition assistance and others lead to more productive and more motivated employees.

6. *Worker safety.* Again, worker safety programs reduce health-care costs, absenteeism, improves retention, morale, and so forth.

7. *Supplier access and viability.* This has been discussed at length in the previous section on stakeholder analysis.

The examples in this chapter are meant to be illustrative of the types of initiatives that some companies undertake in social responsibility, or in creating value. Many more examples can be found in any large firm's website, in its sustainability report.

CHAPTER 10

Renewable Energy and Biofuels

10.1 Introduction

This chapter presents some basic concepts in the area of renewable energy and biofuels, which are key for the reduction of greenhouse gas emissions, both from a policy perspective and from a firm's own sustainability perspective. Figure 10.1 illustrates the energy sources for the electricity generated in the United States in 2016. Renewable energy accounted for roughly 15 percent of all energy generated in the United States in 2016, up from 10 percent in 2010. Electricity generation from wind increased to 5.6 percent from 2.3 percent in 2010, and solar penetration, although only 0.9 percent of all electricity generated in the United States in 2016, increased from 0.03 percent in 2010. This rapid growth rate for wind and solar clearly indicates the increasing importance of renewables in the power generation sector. Figure 10.1 also shows that electricity generated from fossil fuels (natural gas and coal) accounts for 65 percent of all generation in the United States in 2016, and this figure has been relatively stable. What has changed, however, is the increase in natural gas, from 24 percent in 2010 to 34 percent in 2016, followed by the consequent decrease in coal, from 45 percent in 2010 to 31 percent in 2016. Electricity generation from oil is very low in the United States, at less than 1 percent of total. Natural gas is a cleaner fuel source than coal, as indicated in Chapter 4, and discussed further later in this chapter.

In general, only about one-third of the energy content of fossil (or nuclear) fuels ends up as electricity generated to customers. To illustrate, for every 300 kWh of fuel input, 187 kWh corresponds to thermal losses at

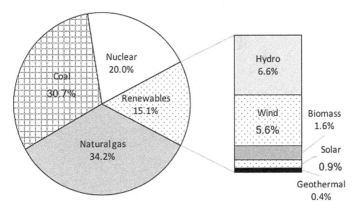

Figure 10.1 Energy sources for U.S. electricity in 2016 (EIA Monthly Energy Review, 2017).

the power plant, 6 kWh is for internal plant use, and 8 kWh corresponds to transmission and distribution losses, and so only 99 kWh of those 300 kWh end up as electricity consumed by users.[1] We explain the origin of these thermal losses in the next section. Of the total electricity consumed by customers in the United States, 37 percent of it go to the residential sector, 37 percent to the commercial sector, 26 percent to the industrial sector, and 0.2 percent going to railroads and other transportation.[2]

The above statistics only include electricity generation and consumption, highlighting the importance of renewable energy sources such as wind and solar. The importance of biofuels is evident when one considers the greenhouse gas emissions in the United States from all different energy sources, including electricity generation, transportation, and heating. Transportation accounts for 38 percent of U.S. greenhouse gas emissions, with almost all of it from petroleum.[3] Because biofuels have the potential to decrease greenhouse gas emissions when compared to fossil fuels, depending on the biomass source (e.g., corn, sugarcane, cellulosic) and production technology as we see later, biofuels are another key element of discussion in sustainability.

To complete this introduction, a quick review of basic physics related to energy and power is in order. Energy, and also work, are measured in joules (J) in the International System of Units (SI). Other units of energy include calories, British Thermal Units (BTU), kilowatt-hour (kWh), and many others. Power is the ratio of energy delivered (or work performed) by a system per unit of time, and it is measured in watts (W) in the SI system:

$$Power = (Energy)/(Time)$$

Thus, in the SI system, 1 W = 1 J/s, or 1 joule per second. The prefixes kilo (k), mega (M), giga (G), and tera (T) refer to multiples of 1000, 10^6, 10^9, and 10^{12}, respectively, of any measurement unit, be it power, energy, time, storage (bytes), etc. Thus, 1 kW is equal to 1,000 W; 1 MW is 1,000,000 W (or 1,000 kW), and so forth. Because Power = Energy/Time, then Energy = Power × Time. As a result, 1 kWh is equal to the energy delivered by a system with power 1 kW = 1,000 W during one hour (alternatively, the energy delivered by a system with power 1 W during 1,000 hours).

10.2   Electricity Generation from Fossil Fuels and Nuclear Power

As discussed previously, fossil fuels and nuclear account for 65 percent and 20 percent of U.S. electricity generation, respectively. As a result, it is important to have a basic understanding of how these types of power plants generate electricity. Figure 10.2 shows, schematically, a **combined-cycle natural gas (NGCC)** plant, including the energy flows. Starting from the top left, fresh air enters a compressor, where it is compressed and then flows to a combustion chamber, where it is joined by the fuel (natural gas). There is combustion, and the hot, high-pressure gas is used to rotate the blades of a gas turbine. The rotating gas turbine is connected to a generator shaft, which then produces alternating current (AC) power. The NGCC plant recovers the heat contained in the hot exhaust gas (over 500°C) exiting the gas turbine through a heat recovery steam generator (HRSG), shown as the box in the center of Figure 10.2. The HRSG transforms water pumped by a water pump into high-pressure steam that is used to rotate the blades of a steam turbine. The exhaust, spent steam is condensed into water, using cooling water (lower right portion of Figure 10.2). The condensed water is then pumped back to the HRSG.

The energy flows in Figure 10.2 indicate that, for each 100 units of energy coming into the NGCC plant through the fuel, approximately 37 are transformed into AC power in the primary generator (connected to the gas turbine), 17 are transformed into AC power in the secondary generator (connected to the steam turbine), 9 are thermal losses from the exhaust gas, and 37 are lost in the condensation and recirculation of the spent steam. The plant depicted in Figure 10.2 has an efficiency of 54 percent (37% + 17%), which is high for a NGCC plant.

The upper part of Figure 10.2, shaded in gray, also shows the basic elements of a **gas turbine** for electricity generation. The gas turbine does not have a HRSG to recover the thermal energy from the hot gas exiting the gas turbine; the hot gas is thus released into the atmosphere, and that thermal energy is lost. Note that, without the HRSG, the efficiency of the gas turbine shaded in gray in Figure 10.2 would be only 37 percent.

A **nuclear power plant** would operate in a steam cycle similar to that shown in Figure 10.2, with the difference that the energy used to generate steam from water originates from nuclear reactions, as opposed to natural gas combustion. Similarly, a coal-fired steam power plant operates under a similar principle, with the difference that in a **coal power plant** the combustion of pulverized coal in a boiler is much "dirtier" than natural gas combustion, and there are considerable pollution control steps to prevent the release of other pollutants. These pollutants include SO_2, which is found in coal and thus becomes a by-product of the combustion, and whose release to the atmosphere is prevented through the use of limestone scrubbers; pollutants also include particulate matter, whose emissions are controlled via electrostatic limestone scrubbers. Pollution controls for coal power plants, such as those descried above, account for almost 40 percent of the cost of building a coal-fired steam power plant.

NGCC power plants require lower initial investments (per MW of power) than a coal-fired steam power plant, and with the current low cost of natural gas, relative to historic standards, they can also be cheaper to operate than coal-fired steam plants. Finally, natural gas power plants release significantly less greenhouse gas emissions than coal-fired steam plants. With all these disadvantages, it is thus not surprising that the fraction of electricity generated by coal in the United States has declined from over 50 percent in the mid-1980s to about 31 percent in 2016, as shown in Figure 10.1.

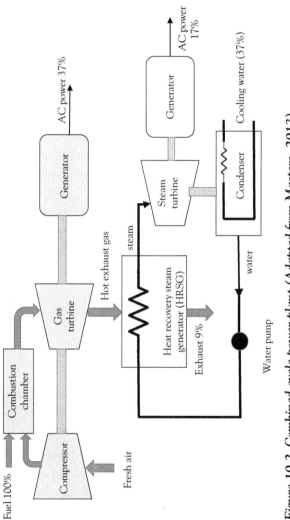

Figure 10.2 Combined-cycle power plant (Adapted from Masters, 2013).

Combined Heat and Power (CHP) plants also operate on a similar principle to the NGCC plant shown in Figure 10.2. The key difference is that the steam generated by the HRSG, shown in the central part of Figure 10.2, is split into two streams in a CHP plant: one for powering a steam turbine to generate electricity (as in the NGCC plant shown in Figure 10.2), and another for heating purposes. The steam can be used for heating buildings, or in industrial processes where heat is needed, such as in paper manufacturing. The percent split between electricity and steam for heating is configured in the design stage. Because hot steam cannot travel too far in steam pipes, due to heat losses, CHP plants are "local," in that they are used to deliver electricity and heat to a subset of nearby facilities, for example, a university, or a processing plant. CHP plants are also typically connected to the grid, which allows them to return unused produced electricity to the grid for some credit, making them even more attractive for a large electricity and heat user. A typical efficiency of a CHP plant (in terms of energy delivered in the form of heat and electricity versus the energy input of the fuel) is 75 percent, which is considerably higher than a NGCC power plant; again, this is because a significant portion of heat is recovered in the form of steam for use in heating, decreasing losses from conversion of steam to electricity.

10.3   Renewable Energy

As shown in Figure 10.1, different renewable energy sources for producing electricity include hydro, wind, biomass, solar, and geothermal. A **hydroelectric power plant** uses a dam to store water, typically from a river, in a reservoir. Water released from the reservoir flows through a turbine and spins it; the rotating shaft activates a generator to produce AC power. Renewable electricity from **biomass** is produced similarly to a natural gas or coal-fired steam power plant. Instead of burning natural gas or coal in a boiler, what is burned are wood chips or other organic residues, such as bagasse from sugarcane. Alternatively, one can also burn biogas originating from a digester filled with organic waste; the gas is generated from the bacteria that digest the waste and produce the flammable biogas. A **geothermal power plant** is similar in principle to a coal-fired steam plant, with the difference that the heat used to produce the steam that powers the steam turbine originates from the earth's core, instead of burning coal in a boiler. In a **wind turbine**, the energy from the wind turns blades around a rotor. The rotor connects to a shaft, which spins a generator to produce AC power, again following the same principle of using some source of energy to spin a generator shaft.

Solar power plants, however, come in two different types. **Concentrated solar power** plants generate electricity by using a system of lenses and mirrors to concentrate a large area of sunlight into a smaller area. The heat produced by this concentrated solar power boils water to produce steam, which powers a steam turbine just like in a coal-fired power plant. The vast majority of solar power, however, comes from **photovoltaic (PV) power stations**, which do not have any movable parts, and they convert energy from light into electricity. Photons are the basic particles of light. Photons with high enough energy and short wavelength may cause electrons in atoms from photovoltaic materials (semiconductors such as silicon, germanium, and others) to break free. If there is an electric field, the electrons move toward a metallic contact, where they emerge as direct current (DC).[4] The DC is transformed into AC through an **inverter**. PV power stations are comprised of several individual rectangular modules. A typical module size is 1.6 m × 0.8 m, with a thickness of 4.6 cm.

In terms of PV technology, there are two types. Traditionally, crystal-silicon-based PV (c-Si) technology has dominated the market, but a more recent type, called thin-film technology has started to emerge. The production of c-Si modules is more capital intensive than thin-film, as it requires silicon processing and wafering stages, and as a result, the c-Si modules are typically more expensive than thin-film ones. In contrast, the *learning rate*—the percentage decrease in cost for every doubling of production—is about 24 percent for c-Si compared to 14 percent for thin-film technology.[5] This means that as the production (and sales) of c-Si PV modules double, the unit cost declines by 24 percent. This learning rate is estimated from regression using historical data, and it is thus an average number of a considerable period of time (since 1976 for c-Si, and since 2006 for thin-film technology). In a nutshell, c-Si technology is more mature, more expensive, but has a higher efficiency than thin-film technology. Efficiency here is defined as the percentage of sunlight energy that the module is able to convert into electricity.

It is fair to say that the most significant growth in renewable energy for electricity production comes from solar and wind power, because they do not emit greenhouse gas emissions during their operation. (From a LCA perspective, there are greenhouse gas emissions associated with the manufacturing of PV modules, inverters, and wind turbines, although those can also be mitigated through the use of solar and wind energy during their manufacturing.) Hydro is constrained by natural resources such as appropriate rivers; it is also emissions free but it does cause some disruptions to natural habitats, beside potentially impacting the local climate. Geothermal is not only emissions free, but it also dependent on geographical characteristics. In contrast, electricity from biomass, although renewable, also emits greenhouse gases, as it involves combustion of organic natural resources. Note that solar power can be installed in rooftops, or it can be installed in large solar farms owned by third-parties or utilities, and it is thus very versatile. In contrast, a wind turbine is not usually viable for residential installation, for example.

The interest and growth in solar and wind can be thus directly attributed to the desire of firms and governments to reduce their greenhouse emissions. Until recently, electricity production from wind and solar could not compete with fossil fuels, and it required different types of incentives, such as tax credits, subsidies, or feed-in tariffs. A **tax credit** is computed based on the overall cost of equipment installed, and then the firm directly claims that tax credit in its final tax bill. For example, suppose the total installed cost of a PV system for a residence, including modules and inverter, is \$105,000. A tax credit (at acquisition) of 30 percent means that the owner can take a tax credit of \$31,500 in the year of installation. In contrast, a **subsidy** would be passed directly from the government to the PV manufacturer, reducing the sales price to the customer. Finally, a **feed-in tariff** is a government-mandated price at which a regulated utility has to buy electricity from a renewable electricity provider; this price is higher than the price of electricity from fossil fuel sources. With the decrease in PV and wind generation costs, some of these incentives have been reduced or phased out entirely, and there are reports of grid-parity in some areas with high efficiencies (think sunny Spain, California or Northern Africa for solar; some coastal areas such as Northern Germany for wind).

The total cost of an installed PV system includes the hardware (modules, inverter, balance-of-system [BOS]), installation labor costs, and other costs such as customer acquisition, logistics, construction, land, overhead, and taxes. Due to the fixed installation costs, larger, utility-scale systems enjoy a lower cost on a unit (per watt) basis. The breakdown and trend of these costs are shown in Figure 10.3 for the residential, commercial, and utility-scale sectors. Notice that the total cost for a residential PV system has decreased from $ 3.11/W in 2015 to $2.93/W in 2016, or a 6 percent decrease in one year. In contrast, the cost of a 100-MW utility-scale system decreased from $1.78/W in 2015 to $1.42/W in 2016, or a 20 percent decrease.

A PV system's power is rated as watt peak, that is, the power in watts delivered under peak insolation conditions. For example, a 1.6 m $\times$ 0.8 m c-Si module might deliver 240 W peak. To find the actual power delivered during, say, one year, one multiplies this rating number by the average efficiency of the solar panel at that particular location. A typical efficiency would be, say, 18 percent for a location with reasonable insolation, such as Los Angeles. This average efficiency figure already takes into account periods such as nights and cloudy days. Considering that Energy = Power $\times$ Time, a 240-W peak module at a location with 18 percent efficiency would be able to deliver in one year (8,760 hours) the following electricity quantity: $(0.18) \times 240 \times 8,760 = 378,432$ Wh, or 378.4 kWh of electricity in one year.

Many residential and commercial PV installations are connected to the grid. If the PV system is not able to meet the entire electricity demand for that location, then the location buys the electricity from the grid (utility) at prevailing rates. If, however, there is excess electricity produced at a particular period, it is then sent back to the grid and the customer may be compensated. The exact compensation amount (in cents/kWh) depends on the jurisdiction, and in some places it can be zero. Some jurisdictions might even force utilities to only charge customers for the net electricity consumed (i.e., total electricity consumed during periods of excess electricity demand minus the total electricity returned to the grid in periods of excess supply). These types of arrangements, commonly referred to as **net energy metering**, incentivize customers to build larger PV systems, in some cases with higher capacity than their demand. If the PV system

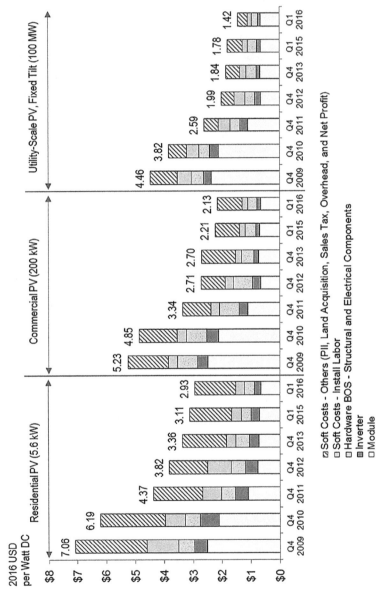

Figure 10.3 Commercial installation costs of PV systems in the United States in 2016. (Source: National Renewable Energy Laboratory)[6]

is not connected to the grid, then the location may use energy storage, such as batteries, to store excess electricity produced by the PV system at certain periods. The battery, however, significantly increases the system cost. In the next section, a simple example is provided where the financial viability of a PV system is estimated.

10.4   Example: Estimating the Financial Viability of a Rooftop PV System

Consider a hotel that wants to install a 200 kW peak rooftop PV system. How does one assess the financial viability of the system? The average efficiency of the system at that hotel location is 18 percent. The initial system cost is $2.5/W peak, including all hardware, construction, and labor costs. However, the jurisdiction offers a tax credit of 30 percent of the investment at the year of installation. Assume that all electricity produced by the PV system is consumed at the hotel, and any excess electricity demand is purchased from the grid. The price of purchasing electricity from the grid next year (the year after installation) is $0.15/kWh, but this figure is projected to increase at a rate of 3 percent per year. Assume that insurance costs are 0.3 percent of the PV system's initial (book value) cost. Finally, the PV system degrades at a rate of 0.5 percent per year. Suppose the PV system is depreciated using a 5-year MACRS schedule, as seen in Chapter 6, with percentages 20 percent, 32 percent, 19.2 percent, 11.5 percent, 11.5 percent, and 5.8 percent for years 1-6, respectively. What is the net present value (NPV) and payback of such a project for a discount rate of 4 percent per year? Consider a 25-year useful life of the PV system, and an income tax rate of 35 percent.

The initial investment of the system (before the tax credit) is 2.5 $/W × 200 kW × 1000 W/kW = $500,000. With the 30 percent tax credit, the cash flow at year zero is − 500,000 + (0.30) × 500,000 = − 350,000. The cash flow in year 1 is as follows. The revenue is the electricity generated times the electricity price. This corresponds to the savings from the PV system, relative to buying electricity from the grid. So, for example, for year 1 the electricity generated is 200 kW × (0.18) × 8,760 h = 315,360 kWh, and thus at $0.15/kWh for the price of electricity, the hotel will save (0.15)(315,360) = $47,304 in electricity in year 1. Insurance cost is

0.3 percent of the initial investment of $500,000, or $1,500. Thus, earnings before tax in year 1 are $47,304 − $1,500 = $45,804. Applying the 35 percent tax ($16,031) results in earnings after tax of $29,773. One then adds the tax savings from depreciation, which is equal to the MACRS percentage (20 percent for year 1) times the depreciation basis ($500,000) times the tax rate (35 percent), yielding $35,000. Thus, the cash flow in year 1 is $29,773 + $35,000 = $64,773.

The changes in cash flows in future years, from year 1, are as follows. In year 2, the electricity produced decreases by 0.5 percent, due to PV degradation, and it is thus 315,360(1 − 0.005) = 313,783, however, the electricity price goes up by 3 percent to 0.15(1.03) = $0.155/kWh, translating into electricity savings of $48,480 in year 2. Insurance cost is still $1,500. The MACRS depreciation percentage in year 2 is 32 percent, which means that the tax savings from depreciation are now $56,000. The cash flow in year 2 is then $86,537. One continues in this fashion until year 25; note, however, that there are no tax savings from depreciation in years 7–25. Using Excel, and the formula -350,000 + NPV(0.04, *cash flows*), where *cash flows* represent the cell range where the cash flows from years 1–25 are displayed/calculated, yields a NPV of $442,727. The project pays back in year 6 (first year where cumulative cash flows become positive).

10.5   Biofuels

We now close this chapter with some basic facts about biofuels. The data displayed here are based on variety of sources, including Petrobras (the Brazilian oil company), several websites, and a United Nations Environmental Programme (UNEP) report.

The two main types of biofuels are ethanol and biodiesel, which are substitutes for gasoline and diesel, respectively, in the transportation sector. The motivation for using biofuels is that the transportation sector accounts for 38 percent of all U.S. greenhouse (GHG) emissions, as previously discussed. Although biofuels are combusted in engines, just like fossil fuels, they have two key advantages: (i) they are renewable and (ii) they can significantly reduce GHG emissions because the crops used to produce biofuels absorb CO_2 during their growth. We discuss this further below. Although biofuels have been used wholly, in many applications they are used in a mix with other fuels. So, for example, E85 means a mix of 85 percent ethanol, and 15 percent gasoline, whereas B5 means 5 percent biodiesel and 95 percent diesel. The energy content of ethanol is 21 MJ/liter, compared to 32 MJ/liter for gasoline. As a result, one needs more than one liter of ethanol to substitute one liter of gasoline. The energy content of biodiesel ranges between 33 and 36 MJ/liter, which is similar to diesel at 36 MJ/liter.

We start with ethanol. The United States is the world leader in the production of ethanol, with 57 percent of the global production of 26.04 billion gallons in 2015, followed by Brazil with 27 percent, and the rest of the world accounting for only 16 percent. The production process for the production of ethanol is shown in Figure 10.4. Sugars are extracted directly from biomass such as sugarcane. One can also use starchy feedstocks, such as corn or soybeans, but one first needs to convert the starch into sugar by adding water (hydrolysis). This is called saccharification, which adds to the cost of ethanol production. Finally, one can also use cellulosic materials for biomass, such as wood and grass—this is called cellulosic ethanol. The process for transforming cellulosic materials into sugar is still rather expensive, and there are limited commercial applications as of now. It is, however, a very promising direction for the future of biofuels. Continuing on the production process, sugars are fermented, resulting in a combination of ethanol and water. Through a first distillation step, 95 percent of the water is removed, resulting in what is called hydrous ethanol. Hydrous ethanol has been used in Brazil as pure fuel since 1978. Another distillation step produces anhydrous (pure) ethanol, which can be blended with gasoline as E10 (what you normally buy at a gas station in the United States as gasoline), or E85.

Compared to corn, sugarcane as biomass has two key advantages. First, ethanol from sugarcane does not necessitate hydrolysis, lowering the production cost. If hydrous ethanol is used as pure fuel, as in Brazil, it also does not necessitate the second distillation, again, lowering the production cost. Second, the productivity of sugarcane is double that of corn for the production of ethanol, in terms of cultivated land area. Specifically, one hectare of land (10,000 m^2) produces on average 82 tons of sugarcane compared to 7.54 tons of corn; one ton of sugarcane yields

77 liters of ethanol, compared to 365 liters per ton of corn.[7] As a result, one hectare of sugarcane yields 6,314 liters of ethanol, compared to 2,752 liters per hectare of corn.

Of course, the production of ethanol, either via sugarcane or corn, requires the use of fossil fuels for agricultural machinery, transportation of feedstocks to the mill, and for the electricity necessary to run the mill. Thus, the comparison requires some LCA thinking; there are roughly four lifecycle stages: cultivation, transportation, production, and use. Cultivation contributes the most, in general, to lifecycle GHG emissions of biofuels. Numbers vary significantly, depending on previous land use (e.g., virgin forest vs. agricultural land), agricultural yield, fertilization and irrigation needs, etc. For example, clearing of virgin forests for the cultivation of feedstocks certainly contributes to significant GHG emissions, potentially negating any reductions in other stages of the life cycle. Transportation (to/from plant) typically contributes the smallest amount, especially if biofuels are distributed in pipelines. In terms of production for corn ethanol, there are wet mills (about 25 percent of all U.S. production), which are larger and capital intensive plants, and modern, more efficient dry mills (75 percent of all U.S. production). The use stage (when biofuels are burned in engines) is generally carbon neutral, because the CO_2 emitted by automobiles and trucks is absorbed by the growing feedstock in a short period of time.

Given all the possible variations in cultivation, production, and transportation, the numbers for **greenhouse gas emissions** of biofuels (compared to fossil fuels) can vary significantly. The *renewable energy ratio* (RER) is the

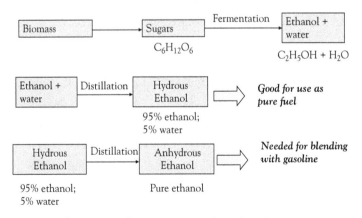

Figure 10.4 Generic production process for ethanol.

ratio of total renewable energy produced per unit of fossil fuel consumed during the life cycle. For sugarcane in Brazil, the average RER is about 9.4, whereas the average RER for corn in the United States is 1.7, although it can be as high as 4.4–5.5 for advanced corn ethanol plants (dry mills) using natural gas, or a CHP.[8] The RER figure does not directly provide the level of reduction in GHG emissions compared to fossil fuels. Estimates of GHG emissions reduction for biofuels compared to fossil fuels are provided in Table 10.1. The data in Table 1 are given in terms of ranges, compiled from many LCA studies, considering that the level of GHG reduction depends on assumptions for cultivation, production, and transportation. Note that ethanol from sugarcane significantly reduces GHG emissions (compared to fossil fuels), with estimates from 70 percent to 143 percent, whereas ethanol from corn has lower reductions, with a maximum of 58 percent. This is not surprising, considering the RER values previously reported. Cellulosic ethanol, while still mostly at the concept stage, is promising also from a GHG emissions perspective, with reductions ranging from 78 percent to 90 percent. Finally, it is interesting to note that biodiesel from palm oil can not only have good GHG emissions reduction, with a maximum of 80 percent, but it can also significantly increase GHG emissions (−800 percent reduction) if virgin forests are cleared and burned for cultivation. Biofuels have also been shown to reduce particulate and hydrocarbon emissions (i.e., local emissions) in many studies.

In terms of biodiesel, the largest producers of biodiesel in the world are, with their production in parentheses, in billions of liters in 2016: United States (5.5), Brazil (3.8), Germany (3.0), Indonesia (3.0),

Table 10.1 Decrease in lifecycle GHG emissions from replacing gasoline/diesel with biofuels

Biofuel	Minimum	Maximum
Ethanol from sugarcane	70%	143%
Ethanol from corn	−5%	58%
Biodiesel from rapeseed	20%	85%
Biodiesel from soy beans	−18%	110%
Biodiesel from palm oil	−800%	80%
Biogas from manure	37%	14%
Cellulosic ethanol (concept)	78%	90%

(Source: UNEP; numbers above 100 percent are possible due to by-products)[9]

Argentina (3.0), France (1.5), and Thailand (1.4).[10] Biodiesel is produced mostly from rapeseed in Europe, and from soybeans in the United States and Brazil. The EU is a large producer and consumer market for biodiesel, because about 50 percent of the price of fuel in the EU is comprised of taxes, and there are significant tax exemptions for biodiesel, as a result of policies to reduce agriculture food surpluses, beside some individual mandates for production and blending with diesel in some member countries.

Of course, biofuels have received criticism as well. For example, in the United States, there are very significant federal subsidies for corn and ethanol production, and most go to large corporations. (There are no subsidies for ethanol production from sugarcane in Brazil.) Further, the production of ethanol from corn in the United States occurs mostly in the Midwest, whereas the largest markets are in the coasts, which increases distribution costs especially because ethanol does not travel well in pipelines of large distances, due to its hygroscopic nature (i.e., it absorbs water). In contrast, in Brazil, production and consumption occur largely in the same geographical areas, especially in the southeastern region. There have also been criticisms of feedstock cultivation for biofuels displacing agricultural or virgin vegetation land. For example, in the United States, there is the displacement of corn for food by corn for ethanol, which can raise food prices and may disproportionately impact the poor. In Brazil, although about 58 percent of the country's production occur in the most populous state of São Paulo, there have been some concerns about the clearing of forests for sugarcane cultivation, especially in the eastern portion of the Amazon forest.

Despite the disadvantages, there are many advantages of biofuels to replace fossil fuels in order to reduce GHG emissions, and to increase energy security. Further, cellulosic ethanol—the second generation of biofuels—is promising, with significant GHG emissions reduction potential as shown in Table 10.1, and of course for the fact that it can use grass, wood chips, or other organic materials that are by-products of other industrial or agricultural processes. For biodiesel, there is also the promising direction for wider use as aviation fuel, since aviation is responsible for 2 percent of all human-induced GHG emissions[11], and commercial aviation is one of the sectors regulated by the EU cap-and-trade scheme.

Notes

Chapter 1

1. Esty and Winston (2006).
2. Cohen (2007).
3. https://www.usnews.com/news/articles/2016-04-22/the-rising-cost-of-recycling-not-exporting-electronic-waste, accessed 05/24/17.
4. https://www2.deloitte.com/content/dam/Deloitte/global/Documents/Technology-Media-Telecommunications/gx-tmt-prediction-used-smartphones.pdf, accessed 05/24/17.
5. http://corporate.walmart.com/global-responsibility/environment-sustainability/sustainable-agriculture, accessed 05/24/17.
6. Toffel and Sesia (2010).
7. http://www.usgbc.org/articles/usgbc-statistics, accessed 05/24/17.
8. Lee and Bony (2009).
9. Reinhardt (1998).

Chapter 2

1. https://www.statista.com/statistics/534898/worldwide-pc-shipments-by-vendor/, accessed 05/24/17.
2. http://ec.europa.eu/environment/waste/weee/index_en.htm, accessed 05/24/17.
3. Atasu and Van Wassenhove (2012).
4. http://www.electronicstakeback.com/promote-good-laws/state-legislation/, accessed 05/24/17.
5. http://www.electronicstakeback.com/wp-content/uploads/Compare_state_laws_chart.pdf, accessed 03/12/12.

Chapter 3

1. Shingo (1985).
2. Bohmer and Ferlins (2006).
3. Peterson and Smith (1998).
4. Gruia and Landel (2008).

Chapter 4

1. Graedel and Allenby (1996).
2. IPCC (2014), http://ipcc.ch/pdf/assessment-report/ar5/syr/AR5_SYR_FINAL_SPM.pdf, accessed 05/24/17.
3. www.ghgprotocol.org.
4. Matthews, Hendrickson and Weber (2008).
5. http://corporate.walmart.com/2016grr/enhancing-sustainability/reducing-energy-intensity-and-emissions, accessed 05/22/17.
6. https://www.epa.gov/sites/production/files/2016-03/documents/stationaryemissions_3_2016.pdf, accessed 05/22/17.
7. https://www.epa.gov/sites/production/files/2016-03/documents/stationaryemissions_3_2016.pdf, accessed 05/22/17.
8. https://www.epa.gov/sites/production/files/2016-03/documents/mobileemissions_3_2016.pdf, accessed 05/22/17.
9. https://www.epa.gov/energy/egrid-subregion-representational-map, accessed 05/22/17.
10. https://www.epa.gov/sites/production/files/2017-02/documents/egrid2014_summarytables_v2.pdf, accessed 05/22/17.
11. http://www.carbontrust.co.uk.
12. https://www.tescoplc.com/tesco-and-society/sourcing-great-products/reducing-our-impact-on-the-environment/, accessed 05/22/17.
13. Corbett, Montes, Kirsch, and Alvarez-Gil (2002).
14. Corbett and Kirsch (2000).
15. Jacobs, Singhal, and Subramanian (2010).
16. Corbett and Kirsch (2000).
17. "LEEDv4 for Building Design and Construction," available at http://www.usgbc.org/resources/leed-v4-building-design-and-construction-current-version, accessed 05/22/17.
18. http://www.usgbc.org/articles/usgbc-announces-23-new-countries-its-leed-earth-campaign, accessed 05/22/17.
19. Miller, Pogue, Gough, and Davis (2009).

Chapter 5

1. Graedel and Allenby (1996).
2. Reinhardt (1998).
3. U.S. EPA (2016).
4. https://www.resource-recycling.com/images/e-newsletterimages/Walmart_Sustainable_Packaging_Playbook.pdf, accessed 06/08/2017.
5. Bras (2010).

6. Bras (2010).
7. Bras (2010).
8. McDonough and Braungart (2002).
9. http://www.c2ccertified.org, accessed 06/08/2017.
10. http://www.c2ccertified.org/products/registry, accessed 06/08/17.

Chapter 6

1. McDonough and Braungart (2002), p. 111.
2. Agrawal and Bellos (2017).
3. Agrawal and Bellos (2017).
4. Agrawal, Ferguson, Toktay, and Thomas. (2012).
5. Agrawal, Ferguson, Toktay, and Thomas. (2012).
6. http://www.interface.com/CA/en-CA/about/modular-carpet-tile/ReEntry-20-en_CA, accessed 05/24/17.

Chapter 7

1. This chapter is modified from an article first published by APICS, Souza (2009). © 2009 APICS.
2. United States International Trade Commission (2012).
3. United States International Trade Commission (2012).
4. http://www.uneda.com/.
5. Ferguson, Guide, Koca and Souza (2009).
6. Guide and Li (2010).
7. Subramanian and Subramanyam (2012).
8. United States International Trade Commission (2012).
9. Abbey, Meloy, Blackburn and Guide (2015).
10. United States International Trade Commission (2012).
11. Abbey, Kleber, Souza and Voigt (2017); Subramanian and Subramanyam (2012).
12. Hauser and Lund (2003).
13. Ferguson and Souza (2010).

Chapter 8

1. Reinhardt (1998).
2. Modified from Reinhardt (1998).
3. Mitchell and Dawar (2008).

4. https://www.ota.com/news/press-releases/19681, accessed 05/24/2017.

5. https://www.energystar.gov/products/how-product-earns-energy-star-label, accessed 05/24/17.

6. https://www.epa.gov/smartway/learn-about-smartway, accessed 05/25/17.

7. http://www.ams.usda.gov, accessed 05/25/17.

8. http://www.ams.usda.gov, accessed 05/25/17.

9. http://www.intertek.com/rohs/walmart/, accessed 05/25/17.

10. http://savedolphins.eii.org/campaigns/dsf, accessed 05/25/17.

11. Worm et al. (2006).

12. https://www.msc.org/about-us/standards/fisheries-standard, accessed 05/25/17.

13. https://www.msc.org/documents/scheme-documents/fisheries-certification-scheme-documents/fisheries-standard-version-2.0, accessed 05/25/17.

14. https://www.msc.org/about-us/standards/chain-of-custody-standard, accessed 05/25/17.

15. https://us.fsc.org/en-us/what-we-do/mission-and-vision, accessed 05/25/17.

16. https://us.fsc.org/en-us/certification/chain-of-custody-certification, accessed 05/25/17.

17. https://www.fairtrade.net/about-fairtrade/what-is-fairtrade.html, accessed 05/25/17.

Chapter 9

1. IPCC (2014); see note 2 below.

2. IPCC (2014), http://ipcc.ch/pdf/assessment-report/ar5/syr/AR5_SYR_FINAL_SPM.pdf, accessed 05/24/17.

3. https://www.gm.com/company/about-gm.html, accessed 06/09/17.

4. https://www.jnj.com/caring/citizenship-sustainability/people, accessed 06/09/17.

5. http://www.businesswire.com/news/home/20150915006063/en/Procter-Gamble-Cleaning-Technology-Deliver-15-Billion, accessed 06/09/17.

6. http://www.nestle.com/csv/communities/coffee, accessed 06/09/17.

7. http://www.tetrapak.com/sustainability/stakeholders-and-reporting/our-partners, accessed 06/09/17.

8. Porter and Kramer (2011).

9. http://sharedvalue.org/about-shared-value, accessed 06/09/17.

10. http://www.coca-colacompany.com/stories/treating-and-recycling-wastewater, accessed 06/09/17.

11. http://www.coca-colacompany.com/stories/setting-a-new-goal-for-water-efficiency, accessed 06/09/17.

Chapter 10

1. Masters (2013).
2. EIA Monthly Energy Review (May 2017), available at www.eia.gov.
3. EIA Monthly Energy Review (May 2017), available at www.eia.gov.
4. Masters (2013).
5. Masters (2013).
6. http://www.nrel.gov/news/press/2016/37745, accessed 06/08/17
7. Donke, Nogueira, Matai, and Kulay (2017).
8. Chum, Warner, Seabra, and Macedo (2013).
9. United Nations Environmental Programme (2009).
10. https://www.statista.com/statistics/271472/biodiesel-production-in-selected-countries/, accessed 06/09/17.
11. http://www.atag.org/facts-and-figures.html, accessed 06/09/17

References

Abbey, J., Kleber, R., Souza, G., and Voigt, G. (2017). The Role of Perceived Quality Risk in Pricing Remanufactured Products. *Production and Operations Management*, 26(1), 100–115.

Abbey, J., Meloy, M., Blackburn, J., and Guide, Jr, V.D.R. (2015). Consumer markets for remanufactured and refurbished products. *California Management Review*, 57(4), 26–42.

Agrawal, V., and I. Bellos. (2017). The potential of servicizing as a green business model. *Management Science*, 63(5), 1545–1562.

Agrawal, V., Ferguson, M., Toktay, L. B., and Thomas, V. M. (2012). Is leasing greener than selling? *Management Science*, 58(3), 523–533.

Atasu, A., and Van Wassenhove, L. N. (2012). An operations perspective on take-back legislation for e-waste. *Production and Operations Management*, 21(3), 407–422.

Bohmer, R., and Ferlins, E. (2006). *Virginia Mason Medical Center*. Harvard Business School Case # 9-606-044, Harvard Business School Publishing, Boston, MA 02163.

Bras, B. (2010). Product design issues. In M. Ferguson and G. Souza (Eds.), *Closed-loop supply chains: New developments to improve the sustainability of business practices* (pp. 39–63). Boca Ratton, FL: CRC Press.

Chum, H., Warner, E., Seabra, J., and Macedo, J. (2013). A comparison of commercial ethanol production systems from Brazilian sugarcane and US corn. *Biofuels, Bioproducts, and Biorefining*, 8(2), 205–223, doi: 10.1002/bbb.1448.

Cohen, D. (2007). Earth's natural wealth: An audit. *New Scientist*, 2605, 34–41.

Corbett, C., and Kirsch, D. (2000). ISO 14000: An Agnostic's report from the frontline. *ISO 9000 + ISO 14000 News*, 9(2), 4–17.

Corbett, C., Montes, M., Kirsch, D., and Alvarez-Gil, M. (2002). Does ISO 9000 Certification pay? *ISO Management Systems*, July–August, 31–40.

Donke, A., Nogueira, A., Matai, P., and Kulay, L. (2017). Environmental and energy performance of ethanol production from the integration of sugarcane, corn, and grain sorghum in a multipurpose plant. *Resources*, 6(1), 1–19, doi:10.3390/resources6010001.

Esty, D.C., and Winston, A.S. (2006). *Green to gold*. Yale New Haven, CT: University Press.

Ferguson, M., and Souza, G. (Eds.) (2010). *Closed-loop supply chains: New developments to improve the sustainability of business practices*. CRC Press, Boca Ratton, FL.

Ferguson, M., Guide, Jr., V.D., Koca, E., and Souza, G. (2009). The value of quality grading in remanufacturing. *Production and Operations Management,* 18(3), 300–314.

Graedel, T., and Allenby, B. (1996). *Design for the environment.* Prentice Hall, Upper Saddle River, NJ.

Gruia, S., and Landel, R. (2008). *Wausau equipment company: A lean journey (A).* Darden Case # UV1079, Darden Business Publishing, University of Virginia, Charlottesville, VA

Guide, Jr. V.D., and Li, K. (2010). Market cannibalization of new product sales by remanufactured products. *Decision Sciences,* 41(3), 547–572.

Hauser, W., and Lund, R. (2003). *The remanufacturing industry: Anatomy of a giant.* Boston, MA, Boston University, Department of Manufacturing Engineering Report. Available for purchase at http://www.bu.edu/reman/OrderAnatomy.htm.

Jacobs, B., Singhal, V., and Subramanian, R. (2010). An Empirical investigation of environmental performance and the market value of the firm. *Journal of Operations Management,* 28(5), 430–441.

Lee, D., and Bony, L. (2009). *Cradle-to-cradle design at Herman Miller: Moving toward environmental sustainability.* Harvard Business School Case # 9-607-003, Harvard Business School Publishing, Boston, MA.

Masters, G. (2013). *Renewable and Efficient Electric Power Systems.* John Wiley & Sons, Inc. Hoboken, NJ.

Matthews, H., Hendrickson, C., and Weber, C. (2008). The importance of carbon footprint estimation boundaries. *Environmental Science & Technology,* 42, 5839–5842.

McDonough, W., and Braungart, M. (2002). *Cradle to cradle: Remaking the way we make things.* New York, NY: North Point Press.

Miller, N., Pogue, D., Gough, Q., and Davis, S. (2009). Green buildings and productivity. *Journal of Sustainable Real State,* 1(1), 65–91.

Mitchell, J., and Dawar, N. (2008). *Nestlé's Nescafe partner's blend: The Fairtrade decision (A).* Ivey Case # 906A20, London, ON, Canada N6A 3K7: Ivey Publishing, Richard Ivey School of Business, The University of Western Ontario.

Peterson, J., and Smith, R. (1998). *The 5S pocket guide.* New York, NY: Productivity Press.

Porter, M., and Kramer, M. (2011). Creating shared value. *Harvard Business Review,* 89:1–2 (January–February), 62–77.

Reinhardt, F.F. (1998). Environmental product differentiation: Implications for corporate strategy. *California Management Review,* 40(4), 43–73.

Shingo, S. (1985). *A revolution in manufacturing: The SMED system.* Portland, OR: Productivity Press.

Souza, G.C. (2009). Remanufacturing in closed-loop supply chains. *Production and Inventory Management Journal,* 45(1), 56–65.

Subramanian, R., and Subramanyam, R. (2012). Key factors in the market for remanufactured products: Empirical evidence from eBay. *Manufacturing & Service Operations Management,* 14(2), 315–326.

Toffel, M., and Sesia, A. (2010). *Genzyme center (A).* Harvard Business School Case N9-610-008.

U.S. Environmental Protection Agency. (2016). *Advancing Sustainable Materials Management: 2014 Fact Sheet.* Report EPA 530-R-17-01.

United Nations Environmental Programme (UNEP). (2009). Towards sustainable production and use of resources: Assessing biofuels. ISBN: 978-92-807-3052-4.

United States International Trade Commission. (2012). *Remanufactured goods: An overview of the U.S. and global industries, markets, and trade.* USITC Publication 4356.

Worm, B., Barbier, E., Beaumont, N., Duffy, J.E., Folke, C., Halpern, B., Jackson, J, Lotze, H., Micheli, F., Palumbi, S., Sala, E., Selkoe, K., Stachowicz, J., and Watson, R. (2006). Impacts of biodiversity loss on ocean ecosystem services. *Science,* 314(5800), 787–790.

Index

Page numbers followed by *f* indicate figures; those followed by *t* indicate tables.

OTHER TITLES IN OUR SUPPLY AND OPERATIONS MANAGEMENT COLLECTION

Joy M. Field, Boston College, *Editor*

- *Understanding the Complexity of Emergency Supply Chains* by Matt Shatzkin
- *Contemporary Issues in Supply Chain Management and Logistics* by Anthony M. Pagano and Mellissa Gyimah
- *Managing Commodity Price Risk: A Supply Chain Perspective, Second Edition* by George A. Zsidisin, Janet L. Hartley, Barbara Gaudenzi, and Lutz Kaufmann
- *Forecasting Fundamentals* by Nada Sanders
- *1+1 = 100: Achieving Breakthrough Results Through Partnerships* by Rick Pay
- *Mastering Leadership Alignment: Linking Value Creation to Cash Flow* by Jahn Ballard and Andrew Bargerstock

Announcing the Business Expert Press Digital Library

Concise e-books business students need for classroom and research

This book can also be purchased in an e-book collection by your library as

- a one-time purchase,
- that is owned forever,
- allows for simultaneous readers,
- has no restrictions on printing, and
- can be downloaded as PDFs from within the library community.

Our digital library collections are a great solution to beat the rising cost of textbooks. E-books can be loaded into their course management systems or onto students' e-book readers. The **Business Expert Press** digital libraries are very affordable, with no obligation to buy in future years. For more information, please visit **www.businessexpertpress.com/librarians**. To set up a trial in the United States, please email **sales@businessexpertpress.com**.

CPSIA information can be obtained
at www.ICGtesting.com
Printed in the USA
BVHW041443070321
601610BV00014B/740